COPING WITH

Verbal Abuse

Janet Grosshandler

THE ROSEN PUBLISHING GROUP, INC. NEW YORK

Published in 1989 by The Rosen Publishing Group, Inc.
29 East 21st Street, New York, NY 10010

First Edition

Library of Congress Cataloguing-in-Publication Data

Grosshandler, Janet.
　Coping with verbal abuse / Janet Grosshandler.
　　p.　　cm.
　Bibliography: p.
　Includes index.
　ISBN 0-8239-0979-4 :
　1. Abused children—Psychology—Juvenile literature.　　2. Psychological child abuse—Juvenile
literature.　　3. Interpersonal conflict—Juvenile
literature.　　I. Title.
　HV713.G75　　1989
　362.7'6'—dc20
　　　　　　　　　　　　　　89-31628
　　　　　　　　　　　　　　CIP
　　　　　　　　　　　　　　AC

Manufactured in the United States of America

For Hank,
My love always.
As I am,
J.

A B O U T   T H E   A U T H O R

Janet Grosshandler is a guidance counselor at Jackson Memorial High School, Jackson, New Jersey. Helping teenagers work through difficult problems in their lives has been a high priority in her life.

Janet earned a B.A. at Trenton State College in New Jersey and followed soon after with an M.Ed. from Trenton while teaching seventh-grade English. Working as a guidance counselor for twelve years has given her a wide range of experience with adolescents. She also writes a weekly newspaper column, "Counselor's Corner," which gives advice to teens and their parents on coping with the ups and downs of the teenage years.

Living in Jackson with her husband, Hank, and their three sons, Nathan, Jeff, and Michael, Janet squeezes in time for running, coaching Little League and soccer, and reading.

Acknowledgments

Many thanks are due to persons who eased my way in writing this book. First and foremost, my love and appreciation go to Hank, my husband, who supports me many times over in all my endeavors.

To my mother, Edna Holstein, who is a source of serenity and strength to me, and who also painstakingly proofread the manuscript, my thanks.

To my sons Nathan, Jeff, and Michael, who let me use the computer to do all this—you always give me the freedom to seek new adventures.

To Ruth Rosen, who opened this first door in the publishing world for me, my sincere appreciation.

I also want to express my thanks to the following counselors and therapists who spent time with me sharing insights: Rosemarie Poverman, Dr. Joann Larsen, Nydia Preto, Steven Schure, Dr. Matthew Schiff, Vickie Wilson, and Esther Ganz. And even though she is not "quoted" in this book, my love to Dr. Ellyn Geller, who started the ball rolling long ago with her faith in me.

And last, but never least, my thanks and appreciation to all the teenagers who share their lives with me so that I can understand their realities and problems. I learn from you every day.

Contents

CHAPTER ◇ 1

Introduction
and Overview

Verbal abuse. Mean, nasty words that wound you to the quick. Sly, suggestive words that make you defensive and wary. Sharp, insulting words that sear your self-confidence. Depending on you, your family situation, and your life, you may be the victim of verbal abuse many times a day.

According to Dr. Joann Larsen, a leading family therapist in Salt Lake City, the average young person receives 100,000 negative messages from parents, teachers, siblings, and peers between birth and the age of twenty. That means that you can be bombarded with over 5,000 negative messages a year!

Dr. Larsen points out that this kind of verbal abuse can promote a negative attitude and low self-confidence. Some psychologists hold that it takes three positive, reinforcing messages to cancel a single negative one. With the use of the put-down so prevalent on television, do you think that

1

most kids receive two or three positive messages to cancel out each negative message they receive?

Where do these comments come from? Who inflicts them on unsuspecting, vulnerable victims? What do you do with them when you receive them? How do you cope with verbal abuse?

This book will take you, the teenager, through various situations in which you will encounter verbal abuse from:

- parents,
- teachers,
- friends,
- bullies,
- siblings,
- boyfriends/girlfriends,
- others,
- and even yourself.

Verbal abusers try to draw you into their game. They attack you with words and wait for you to shoot back the darts, knowing that you'll aim for the heart. This book will give you strategies that you can incorporate into your own life to fend off these attacks while still keeping your dignity and sanity.

"But," you say, "I can't let insults slide by. They'll think I'm a wimp or a coward. I can't let them get away with it!"

First and foremost, adjust your thinking about verbal abusers. These people *like* to make people squirm. It is important for them to see their victims distressed and unhappy.

Why? There's no one reason. Some are just angry at the world. Others have been victims of verbal abuse themselves and are stuck in that pattern of relating negatively to others. Some are insecure and unsure of themselves, and they abuse to reassure themselves that they have power in their limited lives. ✗

Whatever the reason, the abuser expects a certain result: for you to engage in a verbal war that you'll probably lose. So by "not letting him get away with it" you are giving your attacker exactly what he wants. That seems more like letting him get away with it than if you ignore the invitation to verbal sparring.

As long as the plan works for the abuser, he or she will keep right on doing it and you'll keep right on receiving it. You are reinforcing the behavior, and it can become chronic. If you are a fish and a fisherman sends you a juicy morsel of bait on a razor-sharp hook, you have a choice. You can swallow the bait, hook, line, and sinker, in which case you're a goner, or you can swim on to find something more to your liking. If you ignore the fisherman long enough, he'll go away, seeking victims elsewhere.

Rosemarie Poverman is a family therapist who also hosts a Saturday morning radio call-in show. She works with many teenagers individually and with families as a group to help them learn to make decisions that will bring them some happiness and a sense of control in their lives.

"Verbal abuse is very obvious when it's obvious. It's like a slap in the face. Oh my, you call your kid a pig or something like that," Mrs. Poverman says. "But what about the verbal abuse that parents use every day? They do the 'yes buts.' I know you're trying BUT. They can never be pleased. I think that's the kid who's more likely to commit suicide than the one who's acting out his or her anger.

"These kids are injured. They keep holding it in because their parents are basically loving but send the message that they're not good enough."

Mrs. Poverman in her work with teens helps them to

prevent the verbal abuse. "I usually say to a kid that you are responsible for what happens to you. You think you are dealing with your mom who you tell me does these things. If these things make you unhappy—and certainly if these things are true they'd make me unhappy too—then I would try to figure out what it is that makes this happen. And I would try to work my life in a somewhat different way in the hope that this will not happen again."

Mrs. Poverman uses an analogy to explain this. "You go to the same newspaper stand every morning to buy your paper and the man who sells it to you is a real grump who doesn't smile, just grumbles. If every morning you say hello to him in a bright cheery way, you're really not saying hello in a bright cheery way for him. You're saying hello in a bright cheery way for *you*, so that in your mind's eye you look good. If you take his grump, then he owns you and you don't look so good.

"So I say to the kid, look, if you do what's appropriate for you, you look good. You don't have to worry about what other people say to you."

When you do things because you are being verbally abused by your parent or someone else important to you, think about how you make yourself feel when you respond to the harsh words. Do you let yourself get pulled into the pattern of abuse? Or can you concentrate on how *you* want to feel from this encounter and act appropriately?

When you stop doing things that continue a cycle of abuse, you aren't doing it to please the parent, because you'll never please the parent. If you do and say things that make you look good, then you have control.

Another thing is important: Whether it's a parent, a teacher, a brother, a sister, or a friend, you continually need to separate the person from the behavior. That's my father and *that's* crazy behavior. Do you want to react to your father or to the crazy behavior? Mrs. Poverman uses a lot of imaging with the teens with whom she works. Kids need a handle, a way to deal with the abuse sent their way each day. She has them imagine that as they walk down the halls of school or around their house, they have with them a little trashcan on wheels. When one of these things happens to you, put it in your trashcan, because it's garbage and you don't have to keep it.

She advises that you count to ten, take deep relaxing breaths, and imagine yourself taking that stuff and putting it in your trashcan. Later you can dump it. Maybe you'll need a friend to help you dump it.

"Some nice friend will help you take out the trash, or you can come back here and I'll help you dump it. We'll sort through it sometimes, because maybe it's not all trash. Some of it may have a message. Some of it may be legitimate. There's a lot of honesty stuff we can work on."

We tell children, "Sticks and stones will break my bones, but names will never hurt me." If someone is teasing or downright abusing you verbally, the words will hurt *only if you let them.* You have the power to ignore, walk away, or do whatever you can to take the fun out of the attack for the abuser. Don't give him what he wants and expects. Surprise him!

But I'm not that strong, you say. No one has taught me how not to be hurt by my best friend's criticism or my step-father's constant ego-shredding remarks. How do I cope with verbal abuse? This book has game plans for you.

Dr. Larsen, mentioned earlier, believes very strongly in the concept that you are entitled to make mistakes without their reflecting on your own value. You may do something dangerous or stupid, or try out a behavior that is not acceptable. Teenagers do that. That's how you experiment and learn. That's how you figure out how to live your own life separate from your parents.

Is it fair for you to be labeled by a parent, a teacher, a friend, or an enemy because of a mistake or two? No, but it happens sometimes. People use labels all the time. That doesn't mean that the labels are true. You don't have to accept what others say about you.

Let's say a store advertises all kinds of outrageous claims: They have the lowest prices in the world, or they have an exclusive line of "miracle" makeup guaranteed to make you beautiful. Do you have to go to that store? Do you have to believe the advertising hype? Do you have to buy their products, absolutely believing in their "labels"? No, you have choices. You can sort through the gimmicks to see if any of them are true. You can walk by and not even enter the store. Or you can fall for the hype hook, line, and sinker.

One reason you believe the verbal abuse and the labels that are sent your way is that you are at a time of your life when you are working on your own identity. This identity, or self, is separate from your parents, and you are struggling to define just exactly who you are.

Are you a high achiever in school who has to handle lots of pressure? Or are you an average student who is not so concerned with grades, but rather in getting a decent job later on and living a happy life. Do you see yourself as a loser who will never finish high school, or are you working to overcome that?

When you hear criticisms or put-downs from people who are important in your life, especially grown-ups, should you accept all that they say? Are you really what they say you are? Should you give others the power to define your "self"?

One point to remember when trying to cope with those scathing zingers that are shot your way is that the labels people attempt to pin on you are sweeping generalizations. According to Dr. Larsen, labels are the reflection of someone else's negative and limited thought processes. Labels such as wimp, jerk, klutz, fag, and others have more to do with the person giving the label than the person receiving it. Put-downs are part of an erroneous thought process, and they are generalizations, not specific. A label is never one hundred percent true. It is only the way the verbal abuser sees the world, and there are always exceptions to the generalization.

Actually, a person giving out verbal abuse and negative labels is not conveying what is really bothering him. The disapproval reflects more on the giver than on the receiver. It is his or her problem. You don't have to make it yours.

Much of the verbal abuse that abounds in the world has to do with miscommunication. As you read further in this book, you'll see that by investigating and talking out what is happening you can change the scope of the "problem."

For instance, your mother comes home from work and really lays into you about how irresponsible you are and how you can never be counted on to help out. As she criticizes you more harshly, you interrupt to yell, "All I forgot to do was heat the spaghetti sauce in the microwave!"

This then moves the argument into how you are only interested in yourself, you are selfish and never think about her and how hard she works for the family. The two of you work up to some out-and-out verbal abuse, bringing up past problems and blaming each other for most of them.

It ends with both of you storming off and not speaking for the rest of the night.

What is the real problem here? Is the spaghetti sauce the real bone of contention? Probably not, since it can be heated in minutes. By calling a cooling-off period and talking things out with Mom, you might have learned that today she found out about plans for cutbacks in her department, and she might lose her job or have to take a cut in salary.

By communicating and looking for the real reason behind the anger and the verbal abuse, you'll discover that most of the problem lies with the abuser, not with you. Try to be objective, and don't accept the anger and abuse that someone lays on you.

In his book *People Skills*, Dr. Robert Bolton discusses three ways that people relate and communicate with others: by submissive behavior, by aggressive behavior, and by assertive behavior.

People who behave submissively, according to Dr. Bolton, do not respect their own needs and rights. Submissive people don't let others know their feelings, values, or concerns. They allow others to ignore their rights and feelings. When you choose to behave submissively, you may be the object of abuse, verbal or otherwise.

Aggressive people want to overpower others. They push their own needs, feelings, and rights to the forefront at the expense of others. You'll never win an argument with an aggressive person. He'll dominate the entire verbal exchange. Aggressive people are often sarcastic and rude, carrying a chip on their shoulder for others to deal with. These people are the best at verbal abuse.

Dr. Bolton holds that between the extremes of submissive behavior and aggressive behavior lies a middle ground called assertive behavior. The assertive person communicates in a way that does not intrude on someone else's feelings and space. Instead, this person keeps his self-respect and satisfies his needs while at the same time defending his rights, feelings, and values. This type of communicator uses direct and appropriate ways to maintain his own worth and dignity as well as those of the others involved.

Here is a hypothetical situation and three responses. See if you can choose which is a submissive response, which is aggressive, and which is assertive.

Situation: Every time you take an English test your teacher stands at the classroom door and talks loudly with another teacher. Since you sit in the first row near the door, you overhear their entire conversation and lose all concentration on your test. What do you do?

Response #1: You get up and snarl, "Can't you two talk someplace else? No one in here wants to hear your garbage!"

Response #2: You are absolutely furious whenever this happens, but you keep your feelings to yourself and just about fail all your English tests.

Response #3: You speak to your teacher before the next test. You say, "When you and Mr. Smith talk right next to me during the test, I can't concentrate on the answers. Could you hold your conversation for after school? I'd appreciate it."

If you decided that #1 was aggressive, #2 was submissive, and #3 was assertive, you understand Dr. Bolton's continuum of communication behaviors.

Try this *Situation*: Your father often comes home late from work. Tonight you absolutely need to get permission from him to use the boat tomorrow afternoon. You need to get his attention right away. What do you do?

Response #1: Before Dad even takes off his coat, you

plant yourself in front of him and say in a strong voice, "I have to use the boat tomorrow afternoon and I need your okay right now!"

Response #2: You meet Dad at the door, take his coat, and hang it up. When he is comfortable, you say, "Dad, I have something important to discuss with you. It will only take a few minutes. Is now a good time, or should I wait until after dinner?"

Response #3: When your father comes home it doesn't seem like a good time to ask his permission. You wait until after dinner, but then he's in a cranky mood and you hesitate. When your friend calls you later, you tell him that you weren't able to get permission.

#1 is an aggressive communication. #2 is assertive enough to get your father in an open-to-communication mood. In #3 you sacrifice what you want submissively.

Dr. Bolton writes that there are payoffs and penalties for each of these ways of relating to and communicating with people.

Submissive behavior is a way to avoid conflict. It takes two to fight. So by responding submissively to others you can postpone some conflicts in your life. In reality, there are times when this will work for you in dealing with verbal abusers. On the other hand, always being the "nice guy" and letting everyone else call the shots leaves you with some frustration and a life that is controlled by others most of the time.

Aggressive people hold the reins of control on their lives. They go out and get what they want despite the feelings or needs of others. Aggressive people fear the loss of control and often alienate others.

Assertive people can like themselves. They are able to work out problems with others and live their own lives.

Since assertiveness also includes compromise, they learn how to cope and get along with others.

Throughout this book, you will learn various ways to employ assertive behavior when confronted with verbal abuse. You can learn how to keep your self-respect, maintain your dignity, and defend your rights while according those same things to others.

CHAPTER 2

Verbal Abuse

from Parents

Your parents. You love them, and they love you. Then why do you spend do much time fighting and sending each other hurtful messages? You and your parents are running into communication roadblocks. How can you avoid them?

Your parents and you have different needs, desires, goals, and personalities. So conflict will arise. Conflict is difficult to deal with, but you can cut down on the fighting by brushing up your communication skills. Pick up some know-how on talking out your problems rather than engaging in major warfare.

"My last report card was two As, three Bs, and an F. The first thing my father said was, 'Why the F?'" Brad said. "He told me I was stupid and that the failing grade ruined the rest of my report card. Nothing I do seems to satisfy him."

Never pleasing your parents or feeling that you will never live up to their expectations is common. Put-downs from your dad or your mom stick in your throat, making you feel that you could choke. Why do they act like that?

Perhaps they're sending back messages that you've sent them. Lots of kids think their parents don't understand what they are going through and push their parents way into the background. Friends are the only ones who count.

So maybe your parents feel left out, not important in your life anymore. They've gone from being the two most important people in your life to just part of the crowd—or out of it altogether. They may feel unappreciated and unloved, just as you do. Parents may become supercritical or pick fights because they feel ignored.

In Brad's case, his father knew he was having trouble with that particular course, but he never asked for help even though Dad was a teacher himself. If Brad had asked for help and spent some time with his father on the subject, maybe the criticism and subsequent bad feelings could have been avoided.

Try to head off some of the criticisms. Put in some effort to make your parents feel important and included in your life.

"Mom, I love the way you redecorated my room. I know how busy you are with work and the house. I really appreciate it. Could you help me choose some material for a skirt I'm making in home ec class next week?"

"Dad, I know it took a lot of patience to teach me to drive. I never would have gotten my license if you hadn't helped me. Thanks."

What if your parents are overprotective?

"I was sick a lot when I was younger," Maria said. "My father drove me everywhere, made sure I wore my coat, kept me away from other sick kids. I guess he meant well, but now that I can drive he won't let go anywhere! He says I'm not well enough to go on a trip with my girlfriend and her parents. He never lets me use the car alone, and my curfew has always been hours earlier than everyone else I know."

Parents *can* be overprotective and have trouble letting go as you grow through adolescence. Maria's father created a pattern and sends her constant messages that's she's not strong, not well, and can't do much on her own. She's fighting that, but she also doesn't want to cause a major rift with her dad.

What can you do with overprotective parents who are not ready to hand over the reins of your life? How do you react? Do you roll your eyes, put on your angry face, and go into your "I'm not a baby anymore" routine? Telling parents to "Leave me alone" usually triggers a major battle. How can you get what you want without shooting back some biting barbs of your own?

You want to think for yourself, make your own decisions, and spend more time with your friends. Your parents, on the other hand, may wonder whether you can handle situations that could be dangerous. They're not sure whether you will say no to drugs (or say yes). They are afraid you might get too emotionally or sexually involved with your boyfriend or girlfriend. These fears and worries buzz around in your parents' minds and make them crazy, which in turn makes you crazy.

Rather than getting angry at your mom and dad, recognize that if they didn't love you, they wouldn't worry. Try this: "Mom, I know you and Dad worry about me, but you raised me to be careful and level-headed. You've taught me to be responsible, so let me take care of myself a little more and trust my own judgment."

This way you can cool down their concern and show that you can take responsibility for yourself. They can let go of the apron strings. This calm, mature response to parental smothering will give them the message that you are ready to take care of you. Then their verbal put-downs will cease if you follow through on what you say.

Even though your verbal conflict with your parents eases off, sometimes anger flares and open warfare is imminent. You get ready for your parents' criticisms and put-downs. Try to defuse the situation. Say, "I'm so angry now, I'm afraid I'll say some nasty things back to you. I'm going to my room to cool off. Then I'll come back so we can talk this out."

So far this is normal parent/teen stuff. But what about heavy-duty verbal abuse?

"If it weren't for you I would have graduated from college and gotten a decent job!" Mike's mother screamed at him. "Getting pregnant with you was the biggest mistake of my life! I'm still paying for it!"

Mike doesn't have visible scars to show for his mother's attacks, but her constant verbal abuse will mark him emotionally for years.

Twenty-year-old Sandra, not working or attending any school, heard from her father over and over again, "You are such a loser. Look at you! What guy would want you? You better get pregnant by the first guy who comes along so he'll marry you. Then you'll be off my hands."

Verbal abuse from parents usually starts when the children are young, and the message is repeated week after week, year after year. You are no good. You are worthless. You can't do anything right.

"You've got your shoes on backwards. Can't you ever do anything right?"

"You are such a slob! You always spill everything I put in front of you."

"Jimmy is so shy. I don't know what will happen when he starts school. He's afraid of everything."

"You are the child and I am the parent! You don't know anything!"

Out and out verbal abuse at a young age defeats a child's attempt at self-esteem. The message comes across loud and clear.

Sometimes it is subtle. Father introduces son to other adults: "This is my son, the freak," referring to the boy's long hair. "Only kidding," the father jokes it off. But the deed is done. Instant humiliation washes over the son, who has been made to feel like a fool in front of other adults. The invisible scars may never heal.

Sometimes it is downright rude. Mother to ten-year-old after his Little League team lost a game in which he made a mistake or two. "You stink! You missed that easy catch. I couldn't believe my eyes. Get in the car!"

Sometimes you can pass it off: "Yeah, my mother's like that. She doesn't mean anything by it." But most of the time it hurts deeply.

"My mother likes to be told that she looks like my sister," said Allyson, an attractive seventeen-year-old. "But now she's into flirting with guys who come into her store. Last week I was there and this cute guy came in. She told me, 'Allyson, don't call me Mom. Call me Gail.' She didn't want anyone to know I was her daughter!"

In many cases of parental verbal abuse, the parents have the problem, not the kids. The teenagers may assume the blame for the parents' problems because they have been endlessly told that it's their fault. The image of worthlessness seeps into your bones and you may feel that you deserve to be abused.

Not true! That is not the case! You are not to blame for your parents' problems. You did not force your mother to get pregnant and quit college. You are not responsible for your father's insecurities in front of his friends. You are not

VERBAL ABUSE FROM PARENTS

to blame when they get upset over a baseball game. *They are responsible for their own feelings.*

When your parents cannot accept their lives or themselves and heap the blame on you, it can be devastating. In many cases, the situation presents complex problems that cannot be handled within your family. Outside professional help is crucial.

With the help of a competent family or adolescent counselor, plus support from other relatives and friends, you may be able to see your parent for the troubled person he or she really is. Somewhere down the line, your mother or father may have been verbally abused by your grandparent and be just continuing the pattern. Your mom or dad may be carrying anger and hostility from youth and can only express it in abusive ways.

Many teens are afraid to ask for help. You may fear retaliation from your parent for "airing the family's dirty linen" to strangers. You don't want an escalation of the insults to physical abuse.

The first thing to do is to talk to someone. Seek out your clergyperson, a supportive teacher, the school guidance counselor, or a relative who will listen as you speak the unspeakable for the first time. There are also emergency hotlines where you can begin anonymously to receive the help you need.

Taking that first step makes it easier to follow with the second step and get into a counseling program. Ideally, help for the whole family can start you and your parents on the road to acknowledging and dealing with the troubles you face. If you get no cooperation from your parents, get help for yourself.

Counseling can help you put things in perspective. It enables you to step back from the situation and realize that your parent is the troubled one and that you no longer have to carry the burden of blame that you are the one making Mom or Dad miserable.

Your feelings will be mixed up as a result of a long siege of verbal abuse, and you'll need to sort out the turmoil. Will you ever be able to stop blaming yourself? Can you learn to love and trust again? Will you ever be happy?

Each step you take to help yourself will be a stride in self-healing. Your attitude about your life right now and where it is going will make a difference. Many teens survive terrible home situations to live happy, normal adult lives. You can too.

You can do four things to help you through this crisis, to overcome the pain inflicted upon you by an abusive parent.

First, a famous prayer fits here:

Lord, grant me the serenity to accept the things I cannot change, the courage to change the things I can, and the wisdom to know the difference.

People and situations exist in this world that you will never be able to change. Pouring your alcoholic mother's vodka down the sink will not keep her from getting another bottle. You can't wish away your dad's insecurities or feelings of failure. If your abusive parent won't get help to face his or her problem, you can't make it happen.

However, you can work to make changes in your own life. Through counseling and other outside help, you can change the way you react to the situation and learn new coping skills to get you through your present pain.

Second, let go of your parent's problem. Take that step away and separate yourself. The picture you have in your mind of the ideal parent, or the way you want your mom or dad to be does not exist. The painful reality is that he or she is troubled and has emotional problems.

"I watch 'The Cosby Show' on TV and I see how nice the parents are, how they listen to their kids," said fourteen-year-old Mitch. "They don't call them horrible names and curse them out the way my father does. I know. I know it's only TV, but most families are like that, aren't they?"

Mitch feels alone with his problem. He thinks that everyone else's parent is perfect like Bill Cosby. Not so. Many kids share Mitch's problem. He needs to let go of his father's emotional problems. He doesn't need to own the abuse for himself.

Third, you probably want to cause your parent as much pain as he or she gave you. You could spend your life in revenge, prolonging your agony by always wanting to strike back. Some people choose to do this. Perhaps your abusive parent is one of them. These people keep the painful situation alive forever, even after the parent dies. The pattern is perpetuated onto their children.

"I hate my mother for the things she says to me," said Tracy, a high school freshman. "She doesn't scream and yell either, just low-down, sneaky, snide remarks like, 'That dress makes you look fat, doesn't it, honey? Or maybe you gained some weight. When I was your age I worked hard to keep my figure. I guess you don't care how you look.' Then she'll pat my head or something pathetic like that and walk away, leaving me steaming!"

You need to let go of the anger and forgive your parent. Forgive? Yes—forgive, even if it's the hardest thing you'll ever do. If you hold on to your anger, you'll never grow. You'll keep yourself stuck in the pain, mired in revenge and unhappiness.

⟋ Tell yourself that your parent had problems and made mistakes, but that you can leave that behind and grow up to a happier, more positive life. This doesn't mean that all of it didn't matter. In fact it mattered a great deal, which is why you are putting in so much effort to help yourself.

Fourth, find value in *yourself*. After a long period of feeling worthless, it will take some energy to seek out the good inside of you.

In the day-to-day sparring with your parents, you can cope with the great manipulator—criticism—that your mother or father uses on you. As difficult as it is, try not to be defensive. A lot of their criticism comes from their having a hard time dealing with your independence, your need to break away from them and grow up as your own person. They are often confused, upset, and feeling out of control.

Parents feel hurt that you don't want to go places with them anymore and that you tell your best friend things you used to share with them. They feel left out and angry, and they may express those feelings as mean comments or criticism.

They also have a picture of what and who they would like you to be. You have to ease them gently into the real or new you, rather than dropping it like a bombshell. They'll make comments about your hair, earrings, friends, grades, and whatever else doesn't measure up to their vision of you.

Relax. Your parents may be reacting normally just as you are going through the normal growing-up stuff. But there will be skirmishes as you begin to assert your identity and independence.

So try not to be defensive. Don't deny the criticism, and don't counterattack with criticism of your own. That only leads to big arguments, and guess who usually winds up being punished? How often have you heard of a parent being sent to his room and grounded for a week?

In his book *When I Say No, I Feel Guilty*, Dr. Manuel

Smith suggests that you deal with criticism by "fogging." There are three ways to use fogging:

1. Agreeing with the truth in the criticism.
2. Agreeing in principle (with the general idea).
3. Agreeing with the odds.

Parent: "You were late for dinner again."
Teen: "That's true. I was late again" (agreeing with the truth).

Parent: "I bought you that nice winter coat. I can't believe you're stupid enough to go out without it. You'll get sick!"
Teen: "You could be right about that" (agreeing with the principle of the criticism).

Parent: "If you get sick from not wearing that new coat I bought for you, you'll feel terrible and not be able to go out."
Teen: "Right. So when I feel cold enough I'll wear the coat and won't get sick. Then I won't have to stay in" (agreeing with the odds).

Of course, your tone of voice is important. Keep a calm, mature tone when you try out these methods, or your parent may hear you as being fresh and punish you anyway.
Dr. Smith also suggests using negative assertion when someone is pointing out your faults. In negative assertion you agree with the fault and voice their implied criticism.

Parent: "You forgot to turn in your homework again."

Student: "Oh man, I did forget to turn it in again. What an incredibly stupid thing for me to do" (voices the implied criticism).

Stepfather: "Sandy, for a girl with a good shape like yours you sure walk like an Amazon."
Sandy: "I've noticed that myself. I do walk a little funny, don't I?" (takes the wind out of his sails; the criticism becomes meaningless).

In the normal family scene there will be arguments, but keeping lines of communication open with your parents, talking to them outside of times of stress and letting them know that they still figure in your life can go a long way in holding off the arguments.

In times of extreme stress, such as a divorce, job anxieties, death of a close relative or spouse, or life anxieties, parents can be emotionally overwrought. At such times your quest for independence may be stalled for a while until your parents get back on their feet. Family dynamics change during times of extreme stress, so you might need to cool off your anger or chill out your attitude a bit.

CHAPTER 3

Extraordinary

Verbal Abuse

Normal everyday slings from your parent are often the result of their frustration at the moment. Human beings lash out when they need to relieve some pain, and verbal abuse is one of the ways they do it.

But what about heavy-duty emotional abuse with which it is almost impossible to deal? What about a parent who is severely depressed or emotionally disturbed? How about the abuse from a parent who is abusing drugs or alcohol?

"My mother always had her ups and downs," said fifteen-year-old Mandy. "She had been seeing a psychiatrist who had her on medication to stop her mood swings. She would be real happy one minute and then turn mean and ugly the next. She said some horrible things to my sister and me when she was like that."

Mandy was living in a situation over which she had no control. Her mother was not physically or mentally able to control her emotions or to stop verbally abusing Mandy and her sister. This is not a situation in which easy answers fit together like puzzle pieces.

"It's so hard to resolve how I feel about her. I don't think that I'm as demolished emotionally as my sister is. Mom tore her apart so badly that Missy now has no confidence in herself at all."

Mandy, in spite of her mother's unbalanced emotional state, managed to learn to believe in herself and trust her own instincts to help herself and her sister out of that depressing and defeating situation.

"I got help from my aunt. We had Mom admitted to a hospital where she could get the treatment she needed. Then we moved in with my aunt, who gave us space to work out some of the problems that Mom had caused for us."

In a case such as this, you can still love your parent while suffering from the wounds he or she inflicts. You have to make a clear-cut picture of the situation. "This is not really Mom talking to me, saying these terrible things. It is her illness talking. She needs help, not I."

Reach out to others in your family for guidance. This is not something you can handle on your own. If you have no family that can take over, government agencies can help you. You as a teenager do not have to live in such a situation.

Extreme verbal abuse from parents can be caused by other problems. Severe depression may influence their treatment of you. Divorce or the death of a spouse, a parent, or a child may send your father or mother into deep depression.

"When my baby brother died from crib death, my father thought he was responsible because he was baby-sitting while my mother went shopping," twelve-year-old Cori said. "He just snapped out and never seemed to come out of it. He cried a lot about how he let his only son die and that God would never forgive him. It was as if he died too."

Cori's dad went into some real scary black moods. Cori heard him yell at her mother that no one understood how it felt to lose a son. Cori felt hurt, because after all she was still there. Wasn't she good enough even though she wasn't a boy? She was still his child, wasn't she?

Lots of teenagers have to hear and end up believing the verbal abuse thrust at them by parents who are not in control of their emotions or their lives. You suffer from uncertainty and fear of not having a consistent or predictable parent during your teen years. *You are not alone.*

"My mother is a different person since she married my stepfather," thirteen-year-old Stephanie said. "We used to be very close and could talk about anything. Now she hangs on my stepfather's every word and won't make a decision without asking him what he wants. I seem to come in second all the time. I even feel that she doesn't want me around because I might interfere with her new marriage. It hurts a lot. She's so insecure and different. I don't know how to act with her."

When your parent remarries and brings a stepparent into your home, your life changes. Things are not the same as they were with your mom or dad. There's another person in his or her life, and you may feel crowded out a little or a lot. You and your new stepparent need time to adjust to each other and work out a family system of rules and regulations.

"I don't know how to read my stepmother," said fourteen-year-old Cindy. "One minute she's on my side saying that she understands why I did something. The next moment she screams that she's glad I'm not her kid, and if I were she'd ground me for a year. She makes me *crazy!*"

Sometimes dealing with an adult who has never had children takes a special talent. You and your stepparent have no history together and have not evolved any pattern of give-and-take. You also see your real parent saying and doing things that side him or her with your stepparent and against you.

Many of these altercations grow into an exchange of verbal abuse, setting off sparks of indignation and hurt on all sides. How can this be eased so that you are not always on the losing side of the situation?

Some good programs are offered at mental health clinics and at schools for stepfamilies. These programs are designed to teach all members of a blended family new ways of relating constructively to each other rather than lighting a short fuse every time they interact. Communication skills are stressed and practiced so that meaningful solutions to problems can be reached.

"But what about me?" asked Maureen, fifteen. "My mother accused me of trying to turn her new husband on! I wear the same clothes and pajamas and act the way I always used to do before him. He's always looking at me or saying teasing things about me, and my mother goes off the wall. Is he coming on to me or what?"

There is always a possibility of miscommunication in blended families. If you feel that your new stepparent is acting in a sexual way toward you, tell someone. That someone may not be your real parent, since he or she cannot always be objective. You do not have to accept an abusing attitude from a stepparent as part of the marriage deal.

It is also important to examine *your* attitude and actions very carefully. Are you now in competition with your parent? Are you at all responsible for the suggestive communication that is coming your way? If you can honestly say no, and your stepparent is really hassling you verbally or physically, tell someone you trust. You don't want to become another teen who's been sexually abused by a family member. You do not deserve that kind of treatment.

Other kids also have unbalanced family lives over which they have very little control.

"My dad drinks a lot. When he's drunk, we stay away from him. He gets real mean and nasty. We never know what he's going to do or say. . ."

"Mom is a weekend drinker. She waits up for me and drinks. When I get home from my date she starts in with what did I let my boyfriend do and are we having sex. Then she'll call me a whore and accuse me of things I'd never do."

"My stepmother is always zonked out on her tranquilizers. I'm afraid to bring my friends home. I never know what I'm going to find."

If your parents drink or do drugs (prescription or otherwise), what can you do about it? Why do they drink and make life hell for you?

Among adults who drink, one out of ten is an alcoholic, so the chances of your living with an alcoholic parent are pretty high. When your parent is in a drunken or drugged state, he or she can turn on you. How can you deal with that and still have a "normal" life?

First of all, you should learn about alcoholism and drug abuse. Learn more than what you are taught in freshman health class. Seek out full information that will help you get a handle on what is affecting your life.

Alcohol is a drug that affects people in different ways. Some people get silly, dizzy, moody, or confused. Alcoholism is a disease, an illness that causes people to lose control of their drinking habits.

Grown-ups are supposed to have their act together, so why does your parent drink? Maybe your dad feels the need for a few drinks to relax after a stressful day at work.

Perhaps your mother feels the need to dull her senses to make it through the weekend after being divorced.

Parents may want to overcome shyness or fear. They think that drinking will bolster their confidence and make them more appealing to others. Maybe they want to escape problems at work or at home. Some parents need to block out feelings of loneliness or self-doubt.

The more you know about the subject, the less confused you'll be and the better equipped to deal with the ups and downs of your parent's mood swings. Try to help yourself enjoy life and help your family members deal with the problem too. When you are all receiving drunken or drugged verbal abuse, you can support each other.

Usually, abuse starts when a parent is high. Much of the time it is verbal abuse. "I can't stand you kids anymore! You are the reason I drink!" your mother might say. *Not true!*

"You are such a loser. I never thought a son of mine could be so stupid! Get out of my sight before I kill you!" your father may scream in a beer-induced tirade.

How do you cope with this kind of verbal abuse? Those horrible, ripping-apart verbal slashes that catch you unprepared? It's not controllable or coherent most of the time. What can you do to survive this overwhelming attack?

First, as hard as it sounds, *get rid of the guilt.* You are not the cause of your parent's addiction. Alcoholism and drug abuse are diseases that change the way a person thinks, talks, acts, and treats others. You cannot be blamed for that. It's not your fault!

Second, *try not to dwell on your unhappiness.* Easy to say but hard to do, right? It's important to remember that an alcohol problem is not a sign of lack of love. Parents do love you in spite of how they treat you when they are drunk.

Next, *it's okay to be angry.* Are you mad when your mom says horrible suspicious things to you when she's on her pills? Do you get angry at your father when he curses you out when he's drunk? When your parent drinks and hurts you and other members of your family, it's okay to be mad, to feel anger. These are natural feelings, so don't be down on yourself for experiencing them.

You don't have to keep your feelings to yourself. Other kids have the same anger that you do. You can get help from other kids and adults in dealing with the anger, guilt, shame, and helplessness you feel when you're verbally or even physically hurt by an abusing parent.

No matter how bad things become, you can get help in dealing with this kind of abuse. *Talk to someone*—a relative, a teacher, a guidance counselor, a priest, minister, or rabbi. Many schools have special counselors to work with kids who have problems with substance abuse either for themselves or within their families.

Find out more about alcoholism and drug abuse. The more you know, the more you'll understand that what you are feeling is okay. That will help you feel less angry, sad, or helpless about things you cannot change.

Join Alateen or Alanon. Alateen is a self-help group for kids ages ten to eighteen who are living with a parent who has a drinking or drug problem. Alanon is for any family member who is living with an alcoholic or drug-abusing relative. Take your nondrinking parent or your brothers and sisters with you. You'll learn how to deal with your abusive parent. You'll also learn that you are not alone in what you are going through. Excellent help is waiting for you in these groups!

Help others in your family. No one in your family is to blame for your parent's drinking or drug-taking. Offer other family members your love, help, and support.

Take care of yourself. Spend time outside your home with friends: Talk with them and share your feelings. Make new friends. Join a club or special group where you can meet others who have the same interests as you. Check out school clubs, sports organizations, groups at the library, or Scouts.

Take some "me time." Whether it's reading, jogging, or a hobby such as model building, have some fun and enjoy yourself. You are a special person!

CHAPTER 4

Transactional

Analysis for Teens

The first three chapters addressed immediate problems that catch you in the role of victim of verbal abuse. Since parental problems seem to be the most common triggers of verbal attacks, learning ways to deal with your parents and stop the verbal abuse is crucial to your survival and growth.

Adolescents as early as twelve and thirteen want to be recognized as grown-up. Even before the teens kids assert their individuality. But as you get closer to your driver's license and your last years in high school, the drive is really there for you to break away on your own.

In dealing with your parents, you want recognition that you are an adult. However, you may also want to see your parents as though you were still the infant and they the all-giving, all-providing. You are angry at them because they don't always provide what you want.

Rosemarie Poverman, a family therapist, tells teens that if they want to be recognized they must upgrade the relationship between them and their parents. If you want them to start seeing you as an adult, you need to begin recognizing them as adults and not just as parents.

"When I deal with a family in my practice," says Poverman, "I try to demystify or dispel the concept of *the parent.* I can say to a father, 'I understand that your daughter sees you as kind of a rigid person. Is that true?'" He usually says, 'Yes, I am.'

"Then owing to the fact that you have rigid standards, I wonder if we can talk about how people relate to you or how you would like your daughter to relate to you."

Poverman can then explore the interconnected family relationships to sort out what the real problem is and how the family, working together, can come to a fair resolution.

"A lot of what family therapy does is to demystify stuff so that at least we can talk about it. Kids can see their parents as adult persons, separate from themselves, as they learn to project themselves as adults rather than children."

Poverman suggests using the techniques of transactional analysis as a way to cope with an abusive situation, verbal or otherwise. She believes that kids need to be helped to see whether their thinking is logical or illogical.

Transactional analysis is a technical term for a way of communicating with others to get what you want or to solve a problem. How you approach the situation depends on where you're coming from. In transactional analysis, called T.A. for short, you can speak and act from three different perspectives—your CHILD, your PARENT, or your ADULT.

Your PARENT is all the programmed data stored in your brain that was imposed on you and unquestioned by you during the early (birth to five years) stage of life.

These data are recorded straight. There is no editing or

clarification. The data mostly came from your parents or parent substitutes and were sent to you through verbal messages, facial expressions, body language, voice tone, stroking or nonstroking affection, which all add up to rules and regulations.

"Treat others the way you want to be treated."

"You're not old enough to do that."

"Don't eat so much candy. You'll rot your teeth."

"Leave your nose alone," coupled with a light smack to take your finger out of your nostril.

"Always change your underwear. If you have to go to the hospital, you'll want to have clean ones on."

Remember the anger on your parent's face when you broke the living room window?

All that you hear and observe in the first few years of your life is stored in your brain as TRUTH. It is permanent data and cannot be erased. You will replay your PARENT endlessly in life.

Some of the data are rules for survival—"Don't run with scissors in your hand." Others are parental ideas of what's right and what's wrong—"In this family, boys don't cry."

Many PARENT phrases contain "never" and "always." Your PARENT can be good for you or used inappropriately, depending on how it relates to a present situation. Your PARENT is based on outside influences, such as your baby-sitter or teacher or even television.

You have another computer bank that records internal events—your CHILD. What you record in your early years are your *feelings*, your responses to what you see and hear in childhood situations. What is programmed into your CHILD is not exactly what happened but what the child in you felt, understood, saw, or heard.

Since at two months or two years old you didn't have a

big vocabulary to name or place a meaning on what was happening, you had to store the feelings you experienced as you responded to a situation.

You wanted to reach, grab, yell, bang, or explore, and the many messages you got in return were the *no* messages. Those messages gave you some negative feelings that you stored inside you.

As a teen, when you get into a difficult situation your CHILD can surface quickly, and feelings of frustration, anger, and rejection come into focus.

"No, you cannot go to a party where there will be college kids and unlimited beer," your parent says.

"You never let me go anywhere or have any fun. *I hate you!*" you retaliate.

When you are in the throes of these feelings, your CHILD takes over and assumes command. Reason is replaced with anger and irrationality.

However, your CHILD data bank has a good side that doesn't get much recognition. Curiosity, discovery, creativity, laughter, and happiness are all found on the positive side. Stomping through mud puddles, swinging high on swings, holding a squirming, warm puppy for the first time as he plants slobbering kisses all over your face bring into focus the enjoyable feelings in your CHILD.

Unfortunately, for many people the negative responses outweigh the positive, so that when their CHILD emerges in a situation they get the message that they're not okay.

In his book *I'm OK—You're OK*, Dr. Thomas Harris writes that the data in the PARENT and CHILD parts of your brain are all recorded by age five. By then you've been exposed to a multitude of situations, attitudes, and feelings that are translated and stored. They are unreasable and permanent.

Life concepts that are *taught* are stored in your PARENT.

Life concepts that are *felt* are stored in your CHILD. Are you stuck with just these two modes of seeing and responding to the world around you? When someone verbally abuses you, do you trigger off your CHILD or try to clobber the abuser with your PARENT?

Fortunately, you very early start to record in a third data bank: your ADULT, which comes from your own awareness and original thoughts.

When you are young, your ADULT gets put down quickly enough.

Hmmmm, that fish tank looks interesting. I'll just climb up on the table and see what those fish feel like. Maybe I'll even taste those pretty blue stones on the bottom of the tank. . .

"*Get out of that fish tank*! Never put your hand in there, and don't ever put those filthy stones in your mouth!" So much for original thought.

However, as you grow older you do pursue your own awareness of things despite setbacks and obstacles that appear in your way. Your ADULT grows and matures.

Your PARENT judges.

Your CHILD reacts.

Your ADULT figures it out.

Your ADULT can examine your PARENT to see if those data hold true and can be applied to a present situation, or it can check out your CHILD to see if your feelings are appropriate or not.

PARENT: Stay away from bats. They swoop down to bite you and get tangled in your hair. Cover your head with your arms when you see a bat.

CHILD: Bats are disgusting, slimy, scary things. I'm so afraid of them that I scream and run away when I see them.

ADULT: Bats are relatively harmless creatures. They're

probably more afraid of me than I am of them. There's nothing to worry about.

As you approach a situation, you can run through all three of your data banks to decide on an appropriate response. During your teen years you do a lot of testing. You want to check out lots of data stored in your PARENT bank. There may be so much that you feel confused. You can never erase your PARENT or your CHILD, but you can choose to turn off those recordings for a bit.

Use your ADULT to assess the appropriateness of your responses. You don't have to replay inappropriate ones all the time. You can cry at a sad movie; that's appropriate. But if you throw a tantrum and scream at your boyfriend in the middle of algebra class, that's not appropriate. Both responses are stored in your CHILD, but your ADULT can update the information on when to use those responses.

Getting back to the name of all this, transactional analysis, knowing what is stored in all three computer banks will help you "transact" or communicate with others. If you can identify where another person is coming from (PARENT, CHILD, or ADULT), you can form an appropriate response.

In dealing with verbal abuse, you want to know how to deal with the slurs and taunts another person is slinging at you. You want to respond with your ADULT, the data bank that helps you to control the emotional responses and the preachy retorts also. This takes practice and control, in addition to counting up to ten before you answer whoever is heaping out the verbal abuse.

Here's an example of a common situation.

Father: "No, you can't use the car tonight. . . "
You: "I don't believe this! You are so *mean*! You never

let me do anything! You always want to spoil my fun!"

(Your CHILD used in a teenage tantrum usually gets you exactly the opposite of what you want. Listen to yourself when you respond like this, and gauge your parent's reactions.)

Using your logical, careful ADULT response will achieve more of what you want than slipping into your CHILD. Try this approach instead.

Father: "No, you cannot use the car tonight. It's too snowy and slippery out. You won't drive carefully and you'll have an accident."

You: "I appreciate your concern, Dad, but you taught me to drive carefully. There's this special dance at school tonight and I have a date with Nancy. She only lives down the block from school, and I'll use the four-wheel drive so I won't skid."

Dr. Virginia Satir, a famous therapist, has broken down language patterns of people who are under stress and attempting to communicate with others. She established five patterns, which she calls blaming, placating, computing, distracting, and leveling.

People who use the *blaming* pattern put their total selves into it. They invade your personal space by shaking fists or digging into your chest with an index finger. "What is the matter with you?" "Why did you do such a stupid thing?" Sometimes they'll add some sugar. "Honey, couldn't you clean your room once in a while?" (Resembles the PARENT.)

Persons who *placate* are at the opposite extreme from blamers. They are eager to please. They fawn over you, desperate to please you. "Would I mind if you borrowed my homework? Of course not. I only spent a little while on it."

People who use the *computer* pattern are emotionless and program themselves to talk logically and about things in general. Nothing personal. "There's nothing to be scared about." "That's a small problem, nothing that can't be handled." (Resembles the ADULT.)

The *distracter* uses combinations of the first three and tends to panic in the mixture. "Why can't you ever help out around the house? Not that it matters much, you're not here enough as it is. I could be happier if you at least helped with the dishes. But the dishwasher does a good job too. Well, maybe you could do them once a week?"

People who *level* put little emphasis on body language. They say what they have to say and mean it. They don't get as worked up as blamers do, and they do not compute as robotically as the computer pattern. "Why do you smoke pot when you know it's bad for your health?"

The point of these five patterns is that you can spot them pretty easily in a confrontation and decide which pattern to use to answer the verbal abuser.

If you're not sure how to answer an attack or confrontation, try the computer mode. This is a neutral way of dealing with abuse and prevents being a victim.

Classmate: "You'd better let me see your test paper before you hand it in."

You: "It's really interesting that some people think looking at someone else's answers will help them pass the class."

When you turn a computer pattern on someone who is hassling you, he'll be surprised because he will have expected a different answer; either "Okay, okay" or a fight-back "No, I won't let you see my test!" Either way you would have fallen for his bait so he could keep on abusing you.

Your teacher says, "People who want to do well in this class make an effort to hand in their assignments on time."

To keep it from being a verbal attack on you, use the computer pattern of answering: "You're right. Promptness is important in getting a good grade."

Or from your mother: "You know I don't like to interfere, but I think that your recent choice of a girlfriend leaves much to be desired."

"I appreciate your saying that you won't interfere. Other kids' parents get on their case too much."

If you want to practice using your ADULT or your computer mode with a parent or teacher, write down a few remarks frequently made to you by persons in authority. Then write your usual retorts and their reactions. Do you get what you want, or do you get more put-downs that threaten your self-esteem?

Statement #1 (example) Teacher: "You're late to class again."

#2
#3
#4
#5

Next write your usual response to the statement and others' reactions to it.

#1 "Gimme a break, will ya? I'm not that late." (Gets you detention maybe?)

#2
#3
#4
#5

Next write the response you can use from your logical-thinking ADULT.

Response #1 "You're right. Lateness can interfere with learning. I'll make a better effort."

#2
#3
#4
#5

Practice saying these responses before a mirror. Learn to count to five or ten first so you don't rush headlong into a verbal war with your CHILD in control. As you become more accustomed to using these responses, you'll see more success in getting what you want rather than being punished for arguing or fighting.

Transactional analysis or Dr. Satir's modes of communication should give you a better handle on fending off verbal abuse, subtle or strong, by suppressing your immediate inappropriate response and replacing it with a more positive reaction. This will give you the advantage in a communication conflict and help you resolve it to your advantage.

CHAPTER ◇ 5

Verbal Taunts as

Weapons of Anger

Anger. It's a powerful feeling. You've experienced it. Fists clenched. Teeth grinding. Muscles tight. Feeling ready to explode.

Sometimes you know why you are angry. Sometimes you don't. This chapter will help you to understand some of the reasons teenagers get angry. It will help you figure out why your brother dumps his anger and verbal abuse on you, or why your girlfriend snaps at you when you've done nothing to warrant it, or why your new classmate barges in with put-downs and nasty comments. Or maybe you yourself. . .

Teenagers, by your nature, must challenge your dependence on parents, teachers, and the world in general. How can you be independent when you still have to accept so much from Mom and Dad and other adults who have control over you?

You yearn to be on your own, but your physical needs restrict your progress. You're resentful of the authority others hold over you. Anger grows.

So you react. You're not the type to graffiti the principal's office or smash car windows, but you have another weapon—your tongue. Here's your shot at letting off steam and releasing some of that anger. You polish up your arsenal of verbal taunts—against your parents, your teachers, the school administration, the police, government, your friends, your enemies, and everyone else with whom you come in contact.

Do you worry about hurting others' feelings? Heck, no!

What's that you say? You *do* feel bad sometimes after making some insulting remark that you couldn't prevent from popping out of your mouth?

You were embarrassed last week when your clique ganged up and made a total fool out of that nerdy kid?

Oh, you wish you could take back the slew of names you called your little brother at dinner last night?

Okay. All that means is that you're pretty normal. Let's look at adolescent anger and how it causes verbal eruptions that wreak havoc with your relationships with others, not to mention with your guilt system.

LACK OF CONTROL OVER YOUR OWN LIFE

Divorce

The big "D". You found out by eavesdropping or by being in the middle of one of your parents' arguments that one of them was instituting divorce proceedings. One week later your father moved out and started seeing you only on weekends. Two weeks later he moved in with another woman and her child, and you feel you've lost your dad forever.

Mom is complaining about not having enough money, taking her unhappiness out on you and your kid sister. She makes snide comments after you come home from your visit to Dad's "new place" (and new family). You've already heard it from him all day about Mom's faults.

Your sister is harping on how you ate all the cold cuts, and the dog threw up on your bedroom rug. You're ready to explode!

What do you do? Tell off your father in scathing words to give him some of the hurt he's given you?

Insult your mother because she can't get it all together at home anymore and it's wrecking your life?

Berate your little sister because she's an easy victim and you need an outlet for the jumble of feelings inside you?

Kick the dog as you toss the rug out the window?

Punch a few holes in the wall?

Dealing with anger that way complicates your life even more. It's difficult to keep on an even keel, but dealing with your anger in a constructive way will help you retain your sanity.

First of all, find someone to talk to. A friend, your girlfriend's mother, an uncle, your school counselor, a teacher, someone from your church. Having a listener starts to ease the pain right away. It helps to let off the steam building up inside you. Talking doesn't solve your problems, but it allows you to step back and start dealing with your anger.

Keep a journal. Writing about your deepest feelings gives you an emotional outlet and a clearer perspective on what's happening in your life. You don't have to show it to anyone. It's just for you.

Begin an exercise program. Fitness experts and doctors alike agree that aerobic exercise (bike riding, running, brisk walking, cross-country skiing) helps to reduce stress and gives you a more positive outlook on life.

Work on an adjustment in your attitude toward the

divorce. Try to lessen your pain by saying over and over to yourself, "I am a strong person. I can deal with this. I will not let the divorce wreck my life."

If your entire family seems to in difficulties, help to get all of you into a family counseling program. Work for better interpersonal relations and repairing rifts. Give lots of love and support to your family, and you'll get it back.

Moving

Another scary event that makes you feel you have no control over your life is moving. "I'm not going!" may be your first reaction, but you usually have no choice but to go, taking your anger and resentment with you.

"Joanie and I have been going together for eight months now," David said as he sadly shook his head. "How can I leave her and move three states away? I know we'll try to keep it going over the phone and in letters, but sooner or later it'll be over." He pounds his fist into his palm.

"The worst part about moving is losing all my friends," Elaine said dejectedly. "I've known them since I was four years old. How can my parents do this to me? I'll never get that close to anyone ever again!"

Leaving the familiar, the comfortable, the loved feels like ripping your heart apart. You may condense all the hurt into a terrific anger, exploding it all over your family. Your life is not yours to live. The parent dictates, and you seethe with anger.

Use some of those feelings to turn things around for you. Verbally abusing your family will give them the message of how you feel, but will it change the fact that the moving van is coming tomorrow? Probably not.

If you can talk to your family rationally, you can let them know of the hurt and anger. They'll understand and try to help you with it. Ask them to let you come back and visit, to accept a high phone bill the first month, or to let you have a close friend come and stay for a vacation.

If you can accept the fact that you have no choice in the matter of moving, you can turn your energies into making it a positive experience. You can't keep it from happening, but you *can* control how you deal with it.

The hardest part of moving may be leaving your friends. Don't spend all your time dwelling on your loneliness. Instead create a plan to make new friends right away.

- Find out where the local pool or beach is so you can scout out where the other teens hang out.
- Go to the library or community college to see if enrichment classes for teens are offered—an astronomy club, a journalism workshop.
- Get a job in a fast-food place or at the nearest mall. Places that employ lots of teenagers usually need new workers. This can create an instant group of new friends.
- Join a basketball league, a soccer club, or an environmental group. Participate in local five-mile or fun runs. Maybe you'll find someone who needs a running partner.
- Screw up your courage when you approach teens you meet at these places. In your new school talk to your classmates. Say "Hi! I just moved here. There seems to be a lot to do around here. How do you pass the time?"

You'll never forget your old friends; they'll always be a part of you. Your new friends will also enrich your life if you give them the chance.

Money Problems

Lack of money may make you feel that you have little control over your life. You finally have your driver's permit and now your parents expect you to come up with a couple of hundred dollars for car insurance. How could they do that to you? You managed to put some away in your savings account, but that was earmarked for the leather jacket you have on lay-away at the mall.

"My parents don't want me to work a lot of hours during the week because of school," Nick said. "But they expect me to put gas in the car, buy my sisters Christmas presents, chip in for insurance, and pay for my own concert tickets and dates. I can't break even by working Saturdays at the gas station. Either I work thirty hours a week, or they have to ease up on making me chip in for family stuff."

Nick feels caught in a vise. Money is important to just about every teenager, whether the family is affluent or not. But when your parents hold the purse strings tight or expect too much from you, it's time to have a renegotiation conference with Mom and Dad.

Make a list of your day-to-day expenses. Match that with your income, and present a workable plan so that your parents can see you've spent time thinking it through. Rather than delivering verbal barrages about their "stinginess," give them a clear picture of the mature, responsible you. Most parents will respond to that and be willing to renegotiate family finances.

Curfew

Does that word bring a sneer to your lips and an instant knot to your stomach? Do you feel that your parents are unfair and want to ruin your social life when they set the curfew and demand that you adhere to it? Do you shout, slam the door, hurl insults, and use other creative techniques in trying to gain more control over your life?

Try some strategy. Changing an 11 p.m. curfew may seem like moving a mountain with a toothpick. Instead of putting all your energies into angry fights with your parents that only show the immature child in you, observe the curfew for a few weeks. (Right, you'll also have to put up with your friends calling you a baby, right? Tell them it's just part of a plan to influence your parents. They might be interested in that.)

Then choose a special event, a concert or a party that would keep you out later than curfew, and try this: "Dad, Friday night there's a concert at the stadium. Lots of my friends are going, and I have enough money for a ticket. I'm not asking for the car; if you let me go I'll drive with Janice. The concert's not over until 12:30, and then we're going to stop for food. Janice's parents are letting her have the car until 1:30, so I'll be home a little before that. May I go?"

Chances are that by your filling in most of the details, your Dad will be reassured that you have a level head on your shoulders and will extend your curfew.

Compare this method with a slam-bang fight with your parents, with you screaming about how they baby you and them filling you in colorfully on their opinion of you and your friends, along with some harsh words for the group that's doing the concert.

Gaining trust is difficult, but you have to act as if you can be trusted. It's a double-edged sword. You want your parents to trust you, but they don't give you any opportunities to prove your trustworthiness. They lay down rules, regulations, and curfews as if you were a two-year-old climbing all over the furniture.

Acting trustworthy, showing the proof beforehand, and then following through on your promises will go a long way in convincing your father and mother.

UNFAIRNESS OF "THE SYSTEM"

"I can't believe I got detention for being late to classes," Mac complained. "I'm a few minutes late sometimes. School has all these stupid rules. I mean, man, we can't even walk outside the building without getting busted."

Teenagers want to be treated responsibly. You get sick of the rules at home, at school, and in every aspect of your life. Where is the freedom you seek?

Unfortunately, school rules often are made to punish the few who like to break them anyway.

"Since someone pulled a false fire alarm, the entire school will remain for ten minutes past the last bell," your principal's voice booms over the loudspeaker. That means you'll be late for work or the team will start the tennis match without warm-up time because some joker thought it was cool to pull the alarm. He or she is probably off school grounds right now laughing at all of you stuck in class.

New rules, off-the-cuff rules, strict and unfair rules really make you angry. Why won't teachers and principals trust you? Do you walk out of school en masse, refusing to attend classes? That sometimes gets their attention, but not always their cooperation. Again, using your "Just the facts, m'am mentality, draw up a resolution for relaxing some of the unfair rules, and get a group of classmates to present it to the administration.

By acting like responsible people even if they don't give you much chance, you'll probably be able to get some rules changed and you'll earn the reputation of being a level-headed and responsible class. More concessions may come down the line later.

THE NEED TO DECLARE YOUR INDEPENDENCE

Trying to get your parents off your back by being surly and rude won't take you far. In fact, it will probably bring you more punishment and grief than ever. Getting out from under their thumb will come as a result of your proving that you are ready and able to make your own decisions and cope with the consequences of your actions.

"My parents don't trust me an inch!" said Suzanne, age sixteen. "I lied to them a couple of times. I mean, they wouldn't let me see this boy, so I saw him anyway and lied about it. They found out, and now they treat me more like a baby than ever. I hate it!"

Suzanne feels hemmed in, babied, and on a leash. How can she gain the independence she wants? She probably wants to tells her parents off to relieve some of her anger and frustration about not being able to live her own life. What will happen if she really attacks Mom and Dad with a barrage of verbal abuse? Will she accomplish her goal?

Parents and teachers seem to have forgotten what it's like to be an adolescent. You may feel that you have the most old-fashioned parents on earth. Why can't they leave you alone?

Your parents have been taking care of you for a long time. It's a habit. They aren't ready to cut off as the responsible persons in your life. They worry about all the things that happen to teens today: sexual involvement, pregnancy, drug and alcohol abuse, gangs. *They worry*. It's a privilege and a curse.

You can help them to let go and relax their strict outlook by giving them the details of where you are going, with whom, and when you'll be back. Reassure them that they have raised you as a capable and trustworthy person. Ask them how they felt in their quest for independence from their parents. How did they finally get Grandma and Gramps to accept their decisions?

Remind them that you love them and appreciate their love and concern. Acknowledge that you will make a few mistakes, but ask them to accept that this is all part of your experimenting and learning. Arrange a back-up system by which you can call them whenever you really need them. Open up some mature lines of communication with your parents, and your need to resort to harsh words to get your point across will lessen.

Your parents are seeing a different you emerge in these few short years. For a long time you were under their "contol" and they could keep you safe. Now they no longer have that control, and it frightens them. Help them to understand what's going on inside you rather than shutting them out with nasty remarks.

Work for your independence from a mature point of view, but let your parents know that you do still need them, although in a different way.

CHAPTER ◇ 6

Sibling Warfare

"When you see me in school, don't come near
me. I don't want any of my friends to know
you're my brother."

"You are such a jerk. Mom only listens to me. She never
believes anything you say because you lie all the time."

"Don't touch my room, don't touch my bike, don't touch
anything of mine. You break everything, and if I catch you
near my stuff I'll kill you!"

"You'll never be as good as I am, so give up."

Listen to a fight between brothers and sisters sometime,
as an objective listener, of course. Count how many put-
downs are delivered in one go-round. Five, ten, twenty? It
seems that sibling fights are the training ground for shar-
pening your verbal abuse skills. But do you ever think about
the hurt they cause and the damage they do?

Brothers and sisters did not ask to be born into the same
family. They have no choice about who their siblings are,
and some honestly say that they do not like or have nothing

in common with a brother or a sister. Well, whatever fates put you in the same house, unless you move out you have to share your parents, the house, things, and life with kids close to your age.

How do you deal with sibling rivalries, disputes, and negotiations? Do you want to learn how to defuse arguments and help create a win-win relationship with your brother or sister instead of a win-lose war zone?

Some sibling rivalries are staged for the benefit of the parents, a contest for the control of parents, with child number one, two, three, or four coming out on top. Mom and Dad, which of us kids do you love the best?

From the day baby number two comes home from the hospital, the struggle is on to manipulate Mommy or Daddy into showing which child is loved best. This happens in every family. Although the fights may blaze out of control once in a while, minimal emotional damage is done if the parents can show love and approval for all the kids.

In another situation sibling rivalry need be no big deal unless the parents try to overcontrol it. According to Rosemarie Poverman, overcontrol by the parents causes it to escalate out of proportion. "No one's feelings ever get validated, so the frustration goes on and on as family members make louder noises trying to get validated," Poverman says.

Validating is a psychological term that means acknowledging another person, letting the other person know that you heard him, putting no judgment on what he says, and then letting him know where you're coming from.

You may have a family member or sibling who is angry, hostile, and verbally abusive to other members. It's difficult, Poverman agrees, to validate an abusive sibling, but she says, "Most sibling stuff is about validation anyway."

The abusive brother or sister is looking to be validated,

acknowledged for his or her own feelings and viewpoints. If you can turn around your abusive sibling by validating his or her feelings, you can disarm him or her.

For example, brother says to sister, "Your rear end is so big, the whole family could use it as a seat."

Sister has a variety of choice responses:

1. "Your head is so fat, the mush drips out your ears."
2. Slam out of the room, taking the hurt with her as brother smiles with success. Point scored!
3. Punch him, which will give him the excuse to hurt her and release his own pent-up feelings.
4. Other varied but equally ineffective responses.

Or sister can operate from her ADULT, which is hard to do since the CHILD part of the brain snaps into gear faster than the ADULT. Poverman suggests saying to him, "I find what you said really inappropriate. I think more valuable things can come out of your mouth than that." (This gives him credit for saying nice things once in a while and encourages more.)

If she feels strongly, she can say, "You made me really angry when you said that, and I don't like it when you talk to me like that."

Her brother may say, "Well, I really don't care."

She might answer with, "I don't really care that you don't care, but you need to know that." At least she has spoken her feelings and doesn't have to take any hurt with her when she leaves that confrontation.

Always use straightforward stuff. If your younger brother is itching for a fight, you don't have to give it to him. But you *can* say something like, "I don't like you when you do that, so cut it out!"

So simple. So straightforward.

Stay with some validation if you can. "I'm sorry you don't like my choice of clothes, but this is what I'm wearing. If you want a ride, I'm leaving now."

Stick with "I" statements rather than the accusatory "you."

"I get so mad when I hear things like that. Stop it!" rather than, "You are a sorry excuse for a person. You're so hard up." The latter calls for retaliation to defend against your accusations.

Sometimes siblings are the carriers of the family message, Poverman says. For example, Sam teases younger sister Joanne mercilessly. However, Mom has a problem with her own identity as a female and has overidentified with her son, who is her power. So Mom constantly says to Joanne, "Don't bother with what he says. That's the way boys are."

Joanne gets the family message: "Boys can say these things and girls can't. Boys are better than girls and have more power."

If that is what happens in your family, you're going to have a bit of a tough time. Not all families are perfect, and you have a little extra work to do. Try talking to the parent who begins these messages, pointing out calmly (and *not* during a free-for-all argument) that this is the message you are receiving and asking whether it is what he or she really meant to impart.

In day-to-day dealings with your siblings, you need to look at what kind of changes you are willing to make to cool some of the fire-breathing between you.

Dr. Joann Larsen encourages teens to take responsibility for every word that comes out of their mouth. "Everything someone says, the voice tone, volume, cadence, the sound, is the responsibility of the speaker," says Dr. Larsen. "So in an abusive argument with your brother or sister ask yourself, 'Am I contributing to this fight?'"

Most of the time you will answer, "Yes, I am contributing, but he made me do it or she won't let me alone until I scream and yell at her." Hold on to that thought of taking responsibility for your words and actions. Ask yourself, "What can I do to change *me*?"

Dr. Larsen points out that it takes two people to fight. She maintains that all relationships develop patterns and ways of responding to each other, that each actor has a part in the scenario.

"My little sister seems to want to get me in trouble all the time," Marti says. "We have to share a room, and she always has the radio on real loud. As soon as she comes in she turns it up blasting. I scream at her to turn it down. She screams something nasty back. Then Mom comes in and yells at us both. Then I have to go to the den to study if I want silence, and my sister gets our room with the radio. It's not fair!"

Marti's sister readily agrees that she knows just which buttons to push to set Marti off. She has the game plan down pat. Every time she wants the room to herself, she blasts the radio, Marti screams, she returns the noise, and Mom comes in to "settle it." Mom awards Marti the quiet that she wants in the den, when Marti really wants to stay in her room.

Marti and her sister need to look at the game they play. The rules and the consequences of acting on the game plan usually are the same in every fight. Is screaming and verbal abuse and mother acting as referee what they want to continue forever? Probably not.

What kind of home do they want? Are they interested in peace, or do they want a home filled with tension and stress? If Marti and her sister continue this fighting and arguing, they will never achieve peace. However, if lessening of tension and stress becomes the goal, what kind of price is each of them willing to pay?

So we return to, "What can I do to change *me*?"

Dr. Larsen says, "In many relationships, especially between siblings, each one's patterns of behaving and responding are predictable. Each one is as responsible as the other for any sequences that play out more than two responses. Each sibling has control over personal responses that could interrupt the pattern of fighting and arguing."

How can you interrupt your response pattern? When your brother remarks that you'll never get a boyfriend because your face is a mess of pimples, isn't your response pattern predictable? Aren't you giving him exactly what he expects and is waiting for so that he can move along in his pattern of abuse?

"Disengage," says Dr. Larsen. That means not getting pulled into the angry response pattern into which you always fall. Refuse to enter the verbal combat zone where you usually emerge the abused victim. Make a conscious decision not to spend your precious energy on responses that will trigger more verbal abuse.

You can walk away, disengage emotionally, and save yourself anguish and pain.

You can also change the game. Rather than making every interaction with your brother or sister a negative one, switch to a more positive approach. (Remember the question, "How can I change *me*?") Surprise your sibling by doing positive things toward him or her. Offer to lend her a favorite sweater or take him to a movie he's wanted to see for a long time. Give your sister some positive feedback by saying something nice about what she is doing right. Change the scenario in which you communicate with your sibling. Change the game into one where you can both be winners rather than hurt, angry, bewildered losers.

Blood siblings have time going for them. They have spent years together growing up, playing, fighting, loving, hating. But what happens when you become a member of a family that includes stepbrothers and stepsisters?

Having a parent who remarries and gives you a whole other family with whom to interact and communicate can be a mixed blessing. You may wind up with a built-in set of friends. On the other hand, a set of bitter rivals is also a possibility.

"I moved with my mother into my stepfather's house," says fifteen-year-old Lauren. "He already had two sons older than I. I never had older brothers, so I didn't know what to expect." She pauses. "I should have prepared for the worst, because that's what I got. Both of my stepbrothers screwed each other royally to get their father's attention. Then whenever he gave me any attention, I wound up with both the boys trying to slice my heart out."

New stepsiblings have no emotional investment in each other. The family ties that sometimes smooth over rough spots don't yet exist. They have to be built over time. While each stepchild in a newly blended family competes for his own parent's attention and love, stepsiblings may work out frustrations and mixed-up feelings against each other.

Go back to the original question: "How can I change me?" Try to understand that all the kids in a newly blended family are sorting out their own stuff. Do I really belong here? Does my father/mother with whom I live still love me and have time for my needs? Will my father/mother who lives away from me forget all about me? Whom can I count on, and how can I get along in this new family?

Put your energies into accepting your situation. Fighting against a stepfamily won't change much and usually will make all parties miserable. Know that there will be times when you'll have to negotiate, compromise, or back off from what you want.

All family members have different needs, desires, and personalities. Conflict between you and your stepsiblings will happen, but facing the problem and working to resolve it will lead to family harmony and reduce the need for verbal abuse.

Here are some ideas you can put into practice that will avert some of the verbal abuse between siblings or stepsiblings. They are designed to settle conflicts creatively and serve everyone's needs.

Avoid put-downs. Making fun of your brother's, sister's, or stepsibling's ideas, feelings, or physical appearance only causes hurt, resentment, and the urge to retaliate. Even if "He started it," *you* have the choice to end it. Communication gets lost in the bad feelings, and nothing is solved.

Don't "sandbag." If one issue needs to be worked through, stay with that one issue. Whether it is who has the bathroom first or the phone the longest, stay with trying to resolve one issue. Bringing up past problems only builds a wall and blocks any chance of working out whatever is bothering you.

Don't attack. Trying to get off the most biting insult or the most destructive remark as a lead-off to a family discussion or search for solution to an immediate problem demolishes any chance for cooperation and harmony. A load of verbal buckshot will fragment and wound your family members, who may find it difficult to establish trust at the next go-round.

Avoid hidden messages. Say what you mean without cloaking it in garbled messages. If you really want to be alone, say so briefly and clearly. The other person might read you as, "I don't want to be near you" if you shroud your statement with hidden or confusing messages, and bad feelings may result. Remember, as Dr. Larsen says, you should take responsibility for every word that comes out of your mouth and how you speak that word.

What You Can Do

To ward off further verbal abuse from your siblings, you can use "I" statements and be very specific about your objection. "I get upset when I feel you aren't listening to me or caring about what I say," will achieve better results than, "You are a self-centered, selfish jerk! You won't listen to anyone else, you thick-headed brat!"

Use positive statements whenever possible. Let your brother or sister know what is the positive change that you seek. "It would be helpful if I could know in advance when you need the car. Can we work out a schedule for sharing the car without stepping on each other's toes," will be more effective than "You thief! You stole the car just when you knew I wanted it! The next time you want the car, I'm going to take it out from under your nose!"

Discuss problems in a family meeting. Once a month, every week, or if necessary once a day, set aside time when everyone can be together to discuss feelings, conflicts, and changes desired in addition to informing each other of activities and schedules. This is a time to use reason and compromise. If all members insist on getting everything they want, nothing will be accomplished.

Immediate problems that can't wait for a family meeting still need to be resolved at a time when other family members are not tired or distracted. Ruining dinner or waking someone up in the middle of the night will not bring a satisfactory solution to your problem. Plan an appropriate time.

Take responsibility for *your* words and actions. An interaction between two people that takes more than two responses is a shared responsibility. If you have helped create a situation, don't heap all the blame on your brother or sister.

If the conflict and verbal abuse get too intense, *take a break*. Remove yourself, walk away, get away from each other for a cool-down period. Say, "I don't want to fight with you. I'm leaving for a while so we can calm down. I hope we can resume working this out later."

Living and sharing a home with brothers and sisters, step or blood, does not mean that your home has to be a training ground for verbal warfare. Family living takes effort and cooperation from each and every member no matter what age.

It's important to get along with your family. You learn to cooperate, cope, adjust, and meet another human being's needs. Sometimes you have to overlook a lot. These are important imstruments in dealing with the world in general.

Getting along at home is a daily challenge, but the rewards of closeness and honest sharing are worth it.

CHAPTER ◇ 7

Mortifying Words
from Teachers

"**C**hemistry was my hardest subject in high school," nineteen-year-old Janet remembered. "I had a nun who was frightening. Maybe that had something to do with it, because I had this mental block against chemistry from the start. My boyfriend was in my class, so we would do the homework together on the phone every night."

Janet gave a slight shudder and continued. "I'll never forget this one day. I couldn't answer a question when she called on me even though I had spent over an hour on the chapter the night before.

"'Come up to the front immediately!' Sister screamed at me. 'And bring your book!'

"My knees were shaking. I was sure that the other kids could hear my heart pounding. Sister yanked the chemistry book out of my hands and held it open to the homework page, shoving it right in front of my nose. 'Anyone who did their homework would know that answer, young lady,' she yelled, punctuating each syllable by jamming her finger onto the page.

"By then I was so upset that I couldn't have added two plus two. All I could squeak out was 'Yes, Sister' like the polite student I was trained to be.

"'You didn't do your homework!' she intoned, almost gleefully, it seemed.

"Yes, Sister, I did do my homework.

"'No you didn't. Don't lie to me. Go back to your seat.' Sister gave the class a disgusted look, slammed the book shut, and pushed it into my hands as I crawled back to my seat." Janet shook her head.

"I'll never forget that few minutes, and I'll hate that teacher for the rest of my life. I felt humiliated, degraded, stupid, and helpless, and I'll never forgive her for that."

For as many teachers who are nice, sweet, helpful, and supportive, there is that one or possibly two who leave an indelible mark on our souls. They scare us, humiliate us, and use us as a way to vent their frustrations and anger.

Some teachers use verbal abuse in an attempt to be funny. Employed by many middle and high school teachers, sarcasm is meant to make them seem like one of the kids: Make a joke at someone's expense, ha-ha, everyone laughs, and the teacher is cool.

"Most of you did well on this test I'm passing back. It was pretty easy. Except Harvey here. Harvey, you're working hard to keep up that D average, aren't you?" Titters sound around the class as red-faced Harvey slides lower in his seat.

"I don't know what the problem is, Harve, do you?" the teacher asks without waiting for an answer.

"I'm just stupid, I guess," Harvey mutters under his breath.

The adolescent years are a time of insecurity. No one wants to stand out in a crowd, much less be the butt of a teacher's joke. Why do teachers do these things, and what can be done about it?

Although we would like to think that the day of the stern-faced, old-maid schoolteacher is gone, some teachers still rule their classroom by intimidation and disdain. Tread lightly, all ye who enter here, because your ego and self-esteem will be shot to pieces if you don't conform and take what's handed out.

Fortunately, educational movements across the country have been reexamining strategies of teaching and methods of dealing positively with students.

One such program is Teacher Expectations and Student Achievement (T.E.S.A.). Robert Pollock, a middle school principal and former high school assistant principal, is a trainer for this national program.

"The thrust of T.E.S.A. is to examine how equitably students are treated in the classroom. Either consciously or unconsciously, teachers treat low-achieving students less equally either with response opportunities, feedback, or personal regard. These students are treated with anything from disdain to anonymity.

"In T.E.S.A. 'negative codes' are assigned to what we call the mortal sins of teaching, such as sarcastic remarks, undignified put-downs, and the like. We want teachers to examine how frequently they get into these things and change their strategies to dignify all of their students, even the ones that are hard to love."

Teachers are human beings too. They have human emotions, which can run high at times. Teachers can be fearful; there are some real intimidators in the high schools. In the T.E.S.A. program teachers are taught to use strategies to reduce personal conflict with students and to avoid power struggles.

"Teachers who use verbal abuse in the classroom may think they are being funny," Pollock continues. "But a sarcastic remark in the long run turns harmful because you alienate the student, plus a couple of his friends, and even someone else in the class who is thinking that the remark was really unnecessary.

"The tough thing for students to realize is that they will not win a power struggle with a teacher. It's like being pulled over by the police. They want your license and registration and no backtalk. They won't be moved. To a degree, you just have to bite your tongue."

Teachers tend to react to the tones they get. To defuse a tense situation with a teacher, take away the offensive tone from your approach. Remember that an argument takes two to be successful. Remove your half of the power struggle and there will be no fight. You have to be willing to walk away.

"It's like choosing between success and flying your colors high," adds Pollock.

Ninety percent of the time a teacher's negative reaction is not a true indication of his or her feelings. Just as you may dump the weight of the day's troubles on your last-period teacher, so too may a teacher dump his emotions on one person—you. Accept it for the moment without trying to work it out at the point of an argument.

Wait a few hours or until the next day to meet with that teacher after school or at a time when you both can talk. Make it a mirror image and treat that teacher the way you want to be treated. Go in to solve the problem and use low tones.

When you are calm and ready to begin the conversation with your teacher, try an opening statement that will introduce the problem but not in an attacking manner.

You: "Mr. Sommers, I really want to do well in this class, and I especially want to get along with you. Will you give me feedback about how I can do that?"

Now the teacher may not be used to this kind of rational approach and may be surprised and not sure how to answer.

Mr. Sommers: "I don't know what you're talking about. What do you mean?"

You: "It seems that our communication in class has some gaps in it. What can I do to make it better? Could you help me?"

Then Mr. Sommers has the option of pointing out some of the things he sees that hinder your getting along. Since you took a nonthreatening attitude, he should respond in kind. Be open to what he says, since you did ask for feedback. He may have difficulty expressing exactly what he feels is rubbing each of you the wrong way, but sift through his words for some areas in which you can improve. If you show him you are willing to change, you can ask the same of him.

You: "I understand what you're saying, Mr. Sommers. When I come in late and kids call to me when you're trying to settle the class down, it disrupts your plans. I will be here and in my seat before the bell from now on so my friends won't talk to me instead of listening to you."

Mr. Sommers should have no problem accepting your solution to what ticks him off about you at the start of every class. Then you can add:

"This is what would help *me*. Algebra is hard for me, and I don't always get the homework problems right. When you walk around checking the homework, you send me to the board to do one that you see I don't have finished or right. Then I get really embarrassed and flustered, because I feel you want to humiliate me or put me down. Could we work it out so that sometimes I could go to the board with one I have right instead of wrong?"

If you are willing to offer your confessions to the teacher and listen to his or her feedback in a nonthreatening, nonjudgmental atmosphere, you will be able to make *your* request about something you'd like him or her to change. When you offer to change (and follow through on it—no empty promises), the teacher will usually match that offer.

Dr. Joanne Larsen says, "I think the key in working with anyone, teachers included, is to invite rather than demand change. That includes using request skills by asking for what you want rather than complaining about what you are not getting. That is a really powerful tool for people, especially teens, to use."

Invite and request. This is an effective pattern to use. Propose to the teacher what you can do in this class to make things better, and then follow with what would help you in enabling you and the teacher to conduct your business. In addition to what you are willing to change, propose what the teacher needs to change toward you to improve your relationship.

Dr. Larsen suggests that you go a little bit further. Return to the teacher at a later date, maybe two weeks or so, and ask, "How am I doing?" Check out whether he or she perceives that you are holding up your end of the agreement. That will open up more doors for communication.

Usually teachers are receptive to friendly overtures, which you can use even though you may not be feeling very friendly right then. Some people, teachers and students alike, are unapproachable and won't change. But if your approach doesn't work, at least you've tried. You have the option of seeking help from your parents, your guidance counselor, or even the principal.

"The last holdout," Pollock says, "is that you can learn even from teachers you don't like or with whom you don't get along. I learned a heck of a lot from one that I went head-to-head with quite a few times. Don't let your education suffer by concentrating solely on the emotions."

Rosemarie Poverman says, "Teachers wear the cloak of authority. We have to respect them for that. Even if your teachers are abusive, you still have to obey. You may not trust them, but you still have to obey them.

"There's no excuse for a teacher using abusive behavior. Absolutely no excuse. I don't want to say, 'Well, that teacher is having a bad day,' because that's asking the kids to accept that kind of behavior."

Reverting to Poverman's imaging ideas, just take the abusive comment, put it in your rolling trashcan, and throw it out later, because it is garbage, and that's where it belongs.

So often teens say, "That's not fair. Teachers can get away with insulting us, and we get in trouble for telling them off!" That's sometimes true, but usually there are things you can do to change the situation. You don't have to internalize what they've said to you.

Talk to your counselor at school, get your parents involved, change classes, but don't enter into a war with the teacher. It will not help. Check out how others handle this teacher. Does he or she make comments only to you, or is it a common occurrence in the class?

"There's this one teacher in our school," says Frank, a junior in high school. "Everyone warned me about him— that he fails most of his students, that he locks the door on the bell and won't let you in if you're ten seconds late. And I got him. I tried to change my schedule, but I guess everyone was trying to get out of his class; they wouldn't let me change, so I was stuck.

"Now that the year's almost over, it didn't turn out so bad. Yeah, he's strict and wants us to be punctual, but if you learn his point system for grades and do enough work, you'll pass. He sets it up so you know exactly how you're doing, and you can figure out how much work you need for a C or a B. The kids in trouble spend most of their time complaining how tough he is and not handing in work. They're going to fail and have to go to summer school. Not me!"

Sometimes you'll feel helpless. Mr. Jones is your senior English teacher. If you don't pass this required class, you won't graduate. Now English has never been your best subject, but you've managed to squeak by with the help of a tutor.

Mr. Jones is one year away from retirement, and you think he's been out of touch with teenagers for years. He expects the unreasonable—huge amounts of work (sometimes busywork that he makes you do in class while he reads the newspaper).

Writing essays is really not your thing, and he enjoys reading the poor ones aloud in class, criticizing all the mistakes. You get sick to your stomach a half hour before the class begins.

"I've always had problems reading and writing, but this teacher is horrible." Lianne said. "When he wants to make an example of bad writing, he reads mine to the class. It's not just me. He demolishes about ten kids a day."

Lianne tried everything. She had her parent come and talk to Mr. Jones, who maintained that he was going to continue his methods because they had worked for him for thirty years. She went to her counselor to try to change classes, but no other English class would fit in with her schedule. Besides, they weren't transferring any kids out of Mr. Jones's class.

"I got together with kids from all his classes to see if they felt the way I did," Lianne said. "Most of us were tired of being humiliated, and his class was ruining our senior year. We all wanted to learn. I mean, it's probably the last writing class I'll ever have. So we got up a committee of two kids from each of his classes and had a meeting with the head of the English department and the principal."

Lianne and her fellow students presented evidence of the verbal harassment they were receiving and asked for help. The principal and department head were sympathetic and were impressed with their handling of the situation in a mature, rational manner. They promised to look into it.

"When we left that meeting, I wasn't too confident that anything would happen, but at least we had tried."

As it turned out, Mr. Jones did lighten up on his scathing comments about the quality of the students' work. The class became more relaxed when the kids didn't have to prime themselves to fend off the put-downs.

Lianne adds, "The year went by quickly and we didn't dread English class anymore. In fact, we even gave Mr. Jones a little retirement party in our last class, just to let him know we appreciated how he had changed. Maybe we helped him see kids differently."

So if you're feeling helpless about a teacher who just won't quit, approach it from your ADULT perspective. Enlist the aid of others, kids or adults, who will try to improve a poor situation by presenting evidence and suggestions to the powers in charge. You'll come out stronger in understanding, negotiating skills, and cooperation in dealing with what seems to be an impossible situation.

CHAPTER ◇ 8

Verbal

Abuse from Your

Boy/Girlfriend

"I don't know why I stay with him," said soft-spoken, seventeen-year-old Cheryl. "He treats me horribly! When we go out with his macho friends he pushes me around and says disgusting things. I want to hurt him as much as he hurts me, but I still love him. Am I crazy?"

No, Cheryl isn't crazy. Many teens find themselves in a relationship with a verbal abuser who inflicts emotional stress each and every day. The adolescent years are a time of great insecurities. Who am I? How should I act? Will someone love me?

Sometimes getting into a relationship is the answer to your dreams. You are now part of a couple. If she loves you, then you are lovable, which eases some doubts about yourself. Teenagers feel a strong need to belong to and with another person exclusively, but sometimes the dream fulfilled turns into a nightmare.

"I liked this girl a lot, but she was going out with someone else. Then she broke up with him and we started going out. She talked about him and compared us, like, she'd say, 'Joe would never take me to such a cheap place.'

"Then she'd say she was sorry, that she didn't mean it and she loved me, not Joe. I tell you, she has me coming and going. I'm high one minute and in the pits the next. I want to help her. My parents started pressuring me to break up with her. They don't like the way she treats me and the things she says. But I love her."

"But I love her" seems to be the bottom line in many teen relationships. Being "in love" is important, and so many of you are willing to risk pain and emotional abuse in order to stay "in love." You accept the pain as part of the deal and stay in a relationship that is detrimental to your emotional health.

This chapter explores why kids get into and stay with these kinds of relationships. Does love really mean never having to say you're sorry? Is it all right to verbally abuse your boyfriend or girlfriend and expect him or her to understand? Why are certain teens always on the receiving end of verbal abuse from their chosen loves? Does it fit a pattern? How can you change that pattern? Will you be able to find someone who loves you *and* fulfills your emotional needs?

Rosemarie Poverman sees many teenage girls with this type of problem. She says,

"In the typical scenario, mother brings in the daughter because the girl is miserable with the boyfriend but won't break up with him. About one out of fifty might be a depressed young man whose girlfriend has jilted him, but the majority of adolescents I see are the girls."

Mrs. Poverman first determines what is going on with the relationship and whether the girl, because of her own background, is susceptible to emotional abuse.

"To try to help her, I do the opposite of what the parents are doing," Poverman said. "The parents want them apart, want her to break up with him and never see him again. I have no quarrel with that. What I do have a quarrel with is that it doesn't work. How do you keep her out of school where she sees him the most?

"I say to the girl, look, I'm not going to tell you to break up with him. It's not up to me to take charge of your life. I'm only going to ask you if you're here because you're unhappy? Yes, she says. What I'd like to do is help you make yourself happier. Are you willing to work with me for four or six sessions? The answer usually is yes."

The therapist then goes on to teach her some techniques of dealing with the behaviors that upset her the most.

Michelle says, "When I come downstairs dressed for a date, and I think I look good, he'll say, 'You look terrible in those shorts. Take them off!'"

Michelle has a choice to make. Does she go back upstairs and change to make her boyfriend happy? Poverman suggests saying the following:

"I'm sorry you don't like what I'm wearing, but if I'm going out tonight this is what I'm wearing."

By validating the boyfriend's feelings as irrational (I'm sorry you don't like...) Michelle can continue with her statement and still be true to her own opinion that she looks fine. She doesn't have to give control of what she wears to her boyfriend.

Sometimes it takes a stronger statement to get the point across. If the boyfriend is abusive about it, Poverman advises, "Then she can say, 'Look, if you're so upset, I think I'll stay home.' And follow through on that stand."

After a few weeks of this kind of exploration of how she can regain control of her emotional life, she'll probably be talking about not being sure if she wants to stay with him anymore. Then it's *her* choice, not her parent forcing the split.

"You know," Michelle says, "he took me out to this really nice restaurant the other night. I should have been happy, but all I could think about was how gross he looked when he ate." She was fed up with him and working herself up to make a break. A healthy choice.

Sometimes an abusive boyfriend or girlfriend becomes like an addiction. You are locked into the relationship: You know it's not good for you, but you just cannot break it off.

"I've been going with this guy for eight months now," said Nancy. "Either he loves me or he's so mean. He tells me that he doesn't want me with anyone else, then I find out he was at a party with another girl."

Nancy and her addiction fight, make up, fight, make up, and fight again. Her parents have tried to keep them apart and even forbade her to go out, keeping her grounded for the weekends. She sneaked out, lied, and cut school to be with him. They are on the phone until all hours of the night, she believing that her parents don't know she's talking to him.

"I can't live without him," Nancy said. "Sometimes I hate him and how he treats me, but I don't want anyone else to have him."

Nancy needs someone else on her side to help her fight this addiction. She's unhappy, on an emotional roller coaster, and depressed and in despair over this boy. Is that the way she should be spending her teen years?

She could enlist the aid of a younger brother or an older sister to unplug the phone as one step to getting her life back on an even keel. Staying up to all hours of the night makes her oversleep, be late for school, and get in trouble with both school and parents.

She should also get counseling, seeking help to fight off

the addiction and find out why she's continuing to make herself unhappy.

Sometimes the cause is problems in the family. Such situations occur with a child of an alcoholic parent. In a troubled family where all is not normal or emotionally well, kids may be overly abusive or, on the other hand, may tolerate abusive behavior toward themselves.

With the latter type, the family may have set this kid up as the scapegoat for all its problems. Everyone else has unspoken permission to gang up on this one kid, who becomes the recipient of all the anger and frustration. This kid will frequently get into a boyfriend/girlfriend relationship that continues the pattern.

Perhaps your family is functioning poorly, not operating for the benefit of each member's emotional and physical well-being. In such a family unit each member plays a rigid role and communication is severely restricted to statements that fit the roles. You and other members of your family are not free to express a full range of experiences, needs, or feelings. Instead, you limit yourself to playing your assigned role that accommodates those played by other family members.

So when you go looking for love, you turn it into an addiction—something you cannot live without. In Robin Norwood's book *Women Who Love Too Much*, the author cites case after case of women—and men—who are addicted to destructive love.

In general, people who immerse themselves in a destructive relationship probably had little nurturing and their emotional needs were not met within the family. To fulfill those unmet needs, they become exclusive caregivers to needy, emotionally unavailable others.

Like Michelle and especially Nancy, trying to alter your

chosen partner becomes your quest in life. You will do anything to keep him. Your whole life revolves around him, and you believe that the problems in your relationship will be solved if only you try harder or love him more.

You become addicted to emotional pain. Since that is all you have had from your family, you now seek it out in others to keep the hurting pattern going. You know of no other way to love. And even when you change boyfriends or girlfriends you find another one who will continue the pattern.

Your boyfriend may use the power you give him by threatening to leave you if you don't do what he wants. "If you won't have sex with me, I'll find someone who will." You find yourself emotionally blackmailed into doing things you don't want to do; keeping him is the only important thing, so you risk whatever you must so he won't leave you.

Things may get so bad that you feel like killing yourself. "If he doesn't love me anymore, I'll die." You cannot imagine an existence without your destructive love. Your self-esteem is lower than zero, and you cannot exist on your own.

Is this destructive relationship coming from you? Is your boyfriend or girlfriend the one who cannot have a normal love relationship? Is it the combination that makes the addiction so deadly? Whichever the circumstance, you need help to break it.

Where do you find help when you can't change your relationship with an abusive boyfriend or girlfriend? Start with your high school guidance counselor, whom Poverman calls the answer to many kids' prayers; he or she is specially trained to help you.

You might seek professional help. Dr. Matthew Schiff is

a child and adolescent psychologist who has worked with teens involved in addictive relationships.

"I call it the 'Star 80' phenomenon," Dr. Schiff said. Star 80 is the story of a relationship that became so addictive that the man finally shot and skilled the woman who had broken away from his addictive clutches.

"In this type of situation, and I see one or two a year, we are dealing with a fairly sick, unbalanced family or even two families. The youngster cannot end a relationship from which he or she should obviously break away. Often violence follows initial slapping and pushing. Threats occur around issues of jealousy and suggestions of breaking up."

Dr. Schiff cites cases that are seen in the news. Obsession and addiction breed violence and sometimes murder. Something that begins with verbal abuse can change to addiction, jealousy, violence, and the ultimate "breakup" —murder or murder/suicide.

"Separation should take place quickly," Dr. Schiff says. "Therapy is needed because of this pathological relationship. We need to work with the teen to define the relationship and work to get both kids in therapy if possible. The dangers must be pointed out. Watching Star 80 is helpful because often the kids won't take this seriously."

Dr. Schiff strongly warns that such addictive relationships are not to be taken lightly. Teenagers who are so involved have a history of loss and emotional abandonment, in addition to very low self-esteem.

Counseling can help you clarify why you are in this destructive pattern and what it's doing to you.

Working with a therapist can help you find ways to increase your self-esteem and ultimately free yourself from needing this addictive type of love. You don't need to be in constant emotional pain. Love can be sweet and healthy with the right person. If you identify with any of the situations mentioned in this chapter, talk to your school counselor, a trusted adult, or your priest, minister, or rabbi. There are people who can help you start on the road to recovery from your "addiction."

CHAPTER ◇ 9

Verbal Abuse

from Friends

"I'm always late to school," said sixteen-year-old Diana, who had just finished her junior year in high school. "All my life I've had a hard time getting up in the morning and being on time for school. I guess I'm just not a morning person."

Diana's mother had spent years waking her up, cajoling her out of bed, tempting her with her favorite breakfasts, and often driving her late to school. The pattern repeated itself endlessly.

Then Diana's mother changed jobs. She had to leave for work before Diana was ready for school. She was glad to finally be out of the role of Diana's warden.

How did Diana cope with this? She arranged for her boyfriend to drive her to school, so the responsibility of getting her out of the house fell to him—until his parents found out that *he* had been late to school five days in a row. They took away his car keys.

"Jack would scream and yell at me," said Diana. "Call me

lazy and tell me in foul language that I was disorganized. He said I'd be late for my own funeral. He'd nag and nag and threaten to make me walk to school. He sounded just like my mother. I don't need that. So I broke up with him." Jack probably was relieved.

Next Diana enlisted the aid of a girlfriend who took the same bus as she did. Marcy would go to Diana's house fifteen minutes before the bus was due. The job of pushing Diana to get ready faster fell to Marcy, who quit the assignment quickly.

"We only missed the bus twice, and Marcy's mother drove us to school late," Diana explained. But was that a touch of guilt in her voice?

"Marcy was so mad! She told me that I was a lousy friend and that I should grow up and take care of myself. We exchanged some nasty words. She really hurt my feelings."

After a school suspension for being late too often, Diana began to realize that she should have listened to the message between the harsh words. Her mother, her boyfriend, and her friend all tried, albeit through verbal abuse and insults, to force her to be responsible for herself.

What choices did Diana have now? Would she stay the way she was and accept the consequences of her perpetual lateness? If she kept transferring the responsibility to others, she risked receiving more verbal abuse. She could keep on believing the frustrated accusations that she was lazy, irresponsible, and unreliable. She could watch each person give up on her, and that would reinforce her belief that she could not handle her own responsibilities.

Fortunately, Diana faced the problem. She spent time thinking about what the message was and devised a plan to change her pattern of behavior. She took a summer job working with the town's recreation department as a counselor for the children's summer camp program. By getting to bed earlier and buying a *loud* alarm clock, she got up on time.

"I have to get to work even earlier than I'm supposed to be at school. If I'm later than seven-fifteen I'll lose my job. I enjoy working with the kids, and I especially like the paychecks! Maybe school wasn't enough motivation to get up on time, but money works for me."

Diana smiled. "I'm getting away from believing that I'm lazy and irresponsible. My supervisor at camp says I do a great job!"

Because she felt good about her progress, Diana planned for the upcoming school year. "I didn't want to go back to my bad habit when school started. This is my senior year, and I want it to be great! Maybe I'm crazy, but I asked my guidance counselor to schedule me for first-period English class. If I miss that class, I'll flunk. If I flunk, I won't graduate. That should be enough motivation for me to get to school on time."

Would Diana have gotten to this point without some mean words from her friends? Maybe not.

During the teen years, kids listen to their friends more than to their parents. (Perhaps that's why Diana ignored her mother's complaints.) Words from friends are accepted as gospel truth while talk from parents is suspect. Teens are breaking away from dependence on family and replacing it with the closeness of comrades.

That becomes a two-edged sword when you and your friends have a fight. Harsh, insulting words from them hurt deeply. Sometimes spoken in anger, they may carry a message to which you need to pay attention.

"I moved around a lot," said Joe, a trucker's son. "My father is away a lot, but on weekends and vacations I get to go with him. Trucker talk can be pretty raunchy, and I usually carried it over when I went to a new school."

At first Joe paid little attention to his friends who warned him to tone it down, especially around their parents. Since he changed schools often, Joe would just find new friends. Now his parents are divorced, and Joe lives with his mother.

"I'll be staying in this school for the next two years until I graduate. I even have a girlfriend for the first time. I've had to clean up my mouth in order to keep my friends. At first I treated them the way I always did. If they didn't like the way I talk, that's tough. I started getting a reputation, and the kids called me sewer-mouth and worse. But it took a big fight with my girlfriend, who said that her parents didn't want her hanging around with someone like me."

Since Joe wanted to keep his girlfriend and have buddies, he cleaned up his act, not to mention his mouth.

If friends need to send you a message, tell you that you're acting too bossy or that you should change an annoying habit, why don't they say it nicely?

Maybe they have tried. It takes courage to tell your best friend that something he or she is doing is wrong or unacceptable. You risk losing that friend. You might go on dropping gentle hints, trying to find a nice way to tell your boyfriend that you don't like his loud burps in the lunchroom or tell your best friend she is getting too possessive.

When gentle hints don't work, your frustration may erupt and you blurt out, "I hate it when you embarrass me in front of your football friends! If you don't stop, we're through!"

Shock value does get attention. Shouting harsh words lets the other person know how angry you are. (Use it only when it's really needed. If you go around shouting all the time, your friends will tell *you* to can it.)

"Here I was, a football hero, having the best season I'd

ever had. College scouts were coming to see me. I was getting big write-ups in the newspaper. Then wham! I broke my leg. I was so ticked off and afraid my football future was over." Andrew, a senior in high school, spoke with anger and frustration tinging his voice.

"At first I got a lot of attention. My leg was propped straight out in a wheelchair. Everyone fought to be the one to push me around school. But after a while I guess the novelty wore off. I was a has-been, no one special. Gradually the groupies left, and all I had to rely on was my two best friends."

Andrew started taking out his disappointment on them. At first they calmly told him to lay off when he cursed them out or complained about his life. Several times they sat with him, listening to his bitterness and trying to cheer him up to no avail.

"I thought that's what they *should* do. They were my friends, weren't they? I'd have done it for them. Anyway, they were getting pretty ticked off at me, especially Mark. He had three classes with me and took me up and down in the handicapped elevator twice a day."

Finally, Mark's patience reached its limit. After receiving one of Andrew's tirades because Mark had bumped his leg on a locker, Mark gave him back what he had been giving out.

"Now you have to understand that Mark hardly ever curses," Andrew said with a sheepish grin. "So after I told him to watch my damn leg, he left me in my wheelchair in the middle of the crowded hall and loudly told me to watch my own damn leg."

The shock value of Mark's unexpected outburst left Andrew speechless. He had to face the stares of the other kids in the hall and get in and out of the elevator by himself. He quickly realized how good Mark had been to him and that he needed to stop feeling sorry for himself. He got the message, but only after numerous attempts by Mark to show him the light in a less shocking manner.

If you can step back from your anger or the hurt that your friends have given you, you may be able to see a pattern to their message. Then you have to decide to *hear* the message and do something to change your behavior— or you may find yourself with very few friends.

Choose a time when feelings are not running too high, and sit down with one or two good friends. Ask them to give you a clearer picture of what is creating the problems in your relationship. Be ready to hear the complaints, strengthening your resolve to hear the message within the words.

Ask for some suggestions on how to change. Make up a signal that they can use to tell you, "You're doing it again." Be careful not to put the total change on them. *You* have to be the one controlling your behavior and the changes that *you* want to make in order to keep your friends.

On the opposite side of the coin are friends who try to control you. Perhaps they feel little control over their own life and so feel a need to direct yours. Sarah had a friend like that.

"Terri moved in down the street in eighth grade. She seemed older than I, so I fell into tagging along with her and taking all her advice. She told me what makeup to wear, what clothes to buy. She was a little pushy about it, but what did I know? I thought she knew all about that stuff."

It wasn't until Terri talked Sarah into cutting her thick, waist-length hair that Sarah realized how much control of herself she had given up.

"Terri kept telling me that I'd look so much older and prettier with short hair. I always loved my long hair; I was proud of it. But I figured Terri knew what she was doing and she said she was doing it for me, so I let her cut it just before eighth-grade graduation. My mother almost died. *I almost died!*"

Sarah and her mother had a long talk about Terri after that. Sarah came to realize that Terri was not as well-intentioned a friend as she had thought. Terri needed to control others around her, and she did it with sly comments such as, "Do you want to look like a five-year-old?" and "Sarah, that sweater looks horrible on you. It's not your color. Let me wear it and you wear the green one."

Sarah had given up her choices to Terri, losing her self-confidence and identity in the bargain. By means of subtle verbal abuse, Sarah allowed Terri to define her personality, her looks, her *self*.

What could Sarah do? Drop Terri as a friend? Verbally abuse her in return and spread the word that she was a manipulator and had been jealous of Sarah's long hair? Sarah had some tough decisions to make. She felt that Terri did have some good aspects to her personality, but she had been allowing Terri to direct her life choices and thoughts.

"That summer after graduation, I joined a softball team at our local park. I knew Terri didn't like to get her hair and makeup messed up, so she wouldn't play. She tried awfully hard to talk me out of it, saying the other girls were jocks and I didn't want to be one of them if I wanted a boyfriend when we got into high school. But it helped me to make other friends and not be so dependent on Terri for all my decisions."

Sarah also let her hair grow back despite Terri's camouflaged remarks about how ugly it looked long. She realized that Terri wasn't always right and that she could trust her own feelings about herself.

You depend on your friends to reflect and strengthen

your self-image. At times you need them to tell you when they think you're way off base. You can listen to what they say and then make your own decisions about you. You'll have fights and exchange some nasty words in the heat of the argument, but if your friendship is strong and evenly shared you'll be able to help them and they can help you through some tough times in your life.

Be careful not to be completely overshadowed by a friend. You are a worthy human being in your own right, with a lot to give to others. So share your uniqueness, enriching the lives of your friends and adding some specialness to your own.

CHAPTER ◇ 10

Peer Pressure

"**C**ome on. Are you chicken or what?"
"You'll be the only one not going. Everyone will call you a mama's boy if you stay home."
"Grow up! What a baby you are."
"What a wimp! Remind me not to call you when I want to have fun."
"Live a little dangerously. Try this or, I swear, I'll tell everyone how juvenile you are."

Wanting to be grown-up and mature is a large part of adolescence. Kids are smoking, drinking, taking drugs, and having sex earlier in life as a means of trying out "grown-up" behavior. Friends will influence you to do things and try new experiences that you may not be ready for, but it's hard to say no. You risk taunts, insults, and disdain when you don't go along with the crowd or at least with the leader of the crowd.

Cathy's friends started shoplifting at the mall. She felt pretty uncomfortable about stealing the makeup she was urged to take by Allison, the leader of her group. "If I didn't take something, Allison would make fun of me and I would lose all my friends in the group."

Resisting peer pressure, risking taunts, and being branded a coward, wimp, baby, or worse can cause emotional stress and upheaval in your life.

There are ways to fend off this kind of peer pressure. You can learn refusal skills that will keep you safe and out of trouble. Keeping friends is important too, but you will be faced at some point with deciding whether your friendship with someone is worth the risk he or she is trying to make you take.

Peggy, seventeen, had a dilemma. "I really love my boyfriend, but some of the things he does scare me. He's had a couple of accidents and tickets, so right now his license is suspended for a few months. Instead of letting me drive, he insists on driving, even when he's had too much to drink."

"I don't want him to think I'm a coward, and I don't want him to break up with me, but sometimes I wish he wouldn't do those things and expect me to like it."

Wishing someone would change is sort of like wishing you were six feet tall or looked like Debby Gibson. Wishes change nothing. Actions do. Peggy needed to learn to say no to her boyfriend. Otherwise she risked her reputation, her parents' trust, and maybe even her life. Is that what she wanted?

Here are six steps to follow to learn to say no to a pressuring friend. The steps are modeled after a refusal skills training program started by Elliot Herman of Tacoma, Washington. He has trained many people from third grade to high school classrooms, from public schools to juvenile detention centers. After you absorb the ideas, give yourself some practice. It won't be easy to do, but you'll keep yourself safe.

Step 1. Ask questions to find out if you risk getting into trouble.

When Bobby says he "borrowed a car" and wants you to go cruising tonight, you might be suspicious since Bobby's parents took away his license last weekend.

"Come on. Don't be a jerk. We're only going for a ride," Bobby says. Then he turns to others standing around. "This kid is so screwed up and paranoid. He doesn't know if he wants to cruise. What're ya *afraid* of?"

"Nothing," you answer as you meekly get into the car, which could very well be stolen.

Change the scenario to ask questions:

Whose car is it?

Where are we going?

Didn't your parents take away your license last week? Show it to me if you still have it.

Who else is going?

Bobby may be annoyed with the questions and huff off without you. That would be a blessing in disguise, especially if you hear the next day that he got picked up for possession of a stolen car and driving without a license.

Give yourself permission to check things out. Kids who court trouble are doing so to get attention or hurt their parents in some way. Dangerous kids often come from disturbed families and are letting themselves slide into the gutter because they don't believe in themselves or like themselves very much. You don't have to take that sad trip with them.

Kirsten's best friend likes to walk the mall and get picked up by strange guys. Although only fourteen, she looks and acts older and seeks out men in their twenties.

Kirsten has let her friend pressure her into going along

on these "dates." She didn't see much harm in it until the most recent time, when the "guys" turned out to be in their early thirties and drove them to a party two hours away. Kirsten vowed never again, but the pressure is on. Her friend is already planning their next outing.

Kirsten must ask questions to assess the danger she risks encountering. Do we know these guys? How old are they? Are you planning on going in their car? Why do you do this, and why do you need me to go with you?

Kirsten needs to take a stand to keep herself safe. Picking up older guys and driving with them to heaven knows where is risking your life. Kids who flirt with danger usually end up getting hurt. Do you want to be part of that?

Step 2. Put a label on the behavior and use it in talking to your friends.

"We're just going to borrow this for a while. No one will ever know."
"THAT'S STEALING."

"Come on, you wimp, we're just going to the beach for the day. Thay's all."
"THAT'S TRUANCY FROM SCHOOL."

"Just try a little of this pretty stuff. Guaranteed to make you fly. Come on. Do you want us to tell Jenny what a chicken you are?"
"THAT'S DOING COCAINE."

"Sandy's really out of it; she can't drive. You only had a six-pack of beer. You'd better drive us home."
"THAT'S DRUNK DRIVING. NO THANKS."

"Won't the kids in school love us for this? Who else would dare spray-paint Central High's front doors with our school colors? Come on and help me."
"THAT'S DEFACING PUBLIC PROPERTY."

By putting the legal name on the suggested "prank," you bring the situation into perspective. By naming the trouble you could be arrested for, you expose the risk you are taking. It no longer sounds like "fun." It is breaking the law.

Step 3. Identify the consequences of the action.

"If I cut school today, I'll be suspended."
"If I take my parents' car without permission, I'll be grounded for a month."
"If I help you spray-paint the doors of Central High, I could be arrested, have to pay a big fine, and my parents would KILL me!"
"I've had too much to drink. If I get stopped or have an accident on the way home, I'll have to pay a huge fine, probably lose my license, or even go to jail. Not to mention winding up in the hospital or dead."
By impressing on the person what you stand to lose, he or she might realize that the deed isn't worth the risk.

Step 4. Suggest alternative things to do.

"Instead of spray-painting Central High's doors, let's spray-paint huge signs to hang on the fences for the football game next week. The kids will all want to know who did them and we'll be famous! I know where to get the paper."
"I can't drive. I've had too much to drink. My parents

and I worked out a plan under which I can call them, no questions asked, and they'll pick me up. Do you want a ride?"

"I know you lost your license last week. Let's get out the old bikes and cruise down to the beach. It'll get us closer to the girls."

"I'll pass on the cocaine. I'm into health rather than getting high these days. Leave it home. Okay?"

"If you need that CD so badly, I'll lend you the money to buy it. That's better than being caught shoplifting, isn't it?"

An important part of this step is to sell the idea to your friend and then *physically move toward it*. Get out that bike, pick up the phone to call your parents, walk away from the cocaine, or pull out your wallet to lend her the money.

Step 5. If others are going on with the plan, leave.

"If you change your mind, I'll be at home."

"I'm going to class rather than out to the pit for a smoke. See you later."

"I'm going to eat something and have a cup of coffee before I even try to drive. I've had way too much to drink. If I still can't see straight in an hour, I'll call my brother for a ride home. If you want to come with me, I'll be in the kitchen."

"I'm paying for my things now. I'll be at the cash register."

"I'm going home now. If you change your mind, give me a call."

Make it clear that you will not accompany them on the destructive way. Others may forsake the leader and follow you!

Step 6. Give yourself some time and space. Then you may want to make some decisions about your friends.

Is my friendship with Bobby worth all the risks he wants me to take?

If I get caught stealing and Cathy doesn't, is she going to help me out, or am I on my own?

Can I deal with getting suspended from school, arrested, fined, or having a record?

Why are these friends doing these dangerous or illegal things? Why do they want me in on it?

Do I give her power over me?

Are there other kids who could be my friends without pressuring me to do dangerous stuff?

Am I ready to change my friends, risking more verbal abuse?

Do I need help from my parents and family to change my circle of friends?

Am I willing to reach out for more help, counseling perhaps, to change the destructive track I may be running on?

Fending off the verbal abuse and not getting pressured by peers to do something you are not ready for or don't really want to do will take practice and confidence in using these steps.

You might have to enlist someone from your family or another friend who also wants to learn to say no to pressuring, verbally abusing friends. Practice until you have mastered the first five steps so you will feel confident in using them to stand up to a person who is trying to influence you to do something illegal or dangerous.

One high school girl, when discussing the steps, remarked, "But it makes you sound like such a goody-goody. Who wants to be like that?"

A boy who had been picked up for joyriding answered her. "I'd rather be good and alive than super-cool and in jail or even dead."

You can turn the tide, using your own pressure on your peers to keep all of you straight and out of trouble. The refusal skills outlined above will give you some answers when someone asks, "What's the matter? Are you chicken?"

CHAPTER 11

Prejudiced
Verbal Abuse

"**N**o one in our family ever went out with a black boy, Mandy, and you won't be the first."

"Hey, dude, no hablo espagnol in this neighborhood. Understand?"

"Italians are so hot-tempered. Does your boyfriend beat you up when he gets mad?"

"Girls just don't do those things."

"Boys don't cry. Don't be such a baby."

"You're in all those retard classes. You'll never go to college. Who do you think you're fooling?"

"They'll never elect a woman president. Women can't handle world affairs. They'd try to seduce the men leaders, not work with them."

Prejudiced verbal expressions have been in existence for ages and probably will be around for a while longer. Name-calling, unfair and inaccurate labels, and insults abound in this world. Teenagers will hear them from their parents and friends, in movies, on television, and from other sources. They're a fact of life. Suspicious, bullying people need to put others down to meet their own need to feel superior.

"We were the first black family to move to this side of town," said Sandra, a junior in high school. "We already knew most of the kids from school, so they weren't really any problem. But the grown-ups! A few of the men in the neighborhood said nasty things to my younger brothers, like knowing whom to blame if their hubcaps were stolen. Can you imagine that? It was the adults who couldn't handle it."

Sandra's family met prejudiced verbal abuse early in the new neighborhood. Adults, acting on misinformation and fear, verbally threatened her brothers, instigating even more bad feelings.

One of the hardest things in the world is to change people and their lifelong beliefs. You don't know their history and how they came to be so prejudiced. Racial prejudice comes from lumping an entire group of people into one narrow category, making no allowance for individual differences, ambitions, attitudes, family life, or other factors.

The following are some of the prejudiced remarks that ignorant people spout each day:

All Cubans are drug dealers.
All blacks have criminal tendencies.
All Haitians have AIDS.
All Italians have hot tempers.
All Polish people are dumb.
Kids with learning disabilities will never be successful and should drop out of school.
Females are good for only one thing—sex. They can't

run a business or do what men do. If you point out a woman who does those things, she must be a lesbian who wishes she was a man.

These "all or none" statements feed people's fears and cause them to keep on spreading the prejudice. Do you ever wonder why these verbal abusers will not accept evidence that would demolish their beliefs? Perhaps they feel safe in their ignorance and are not willing to give up that safety no matter whom it hurts.

Ethnic jokes abound as prejudiced people air their beliefs and apply unfair and inaccurate labels. Even people who say they are not prejudiced will tell Polish jokes or make anti-black remarks. Is it in the name of humor that people feel the need to smear a person's heritage or specialness?

"When kids make jokes about how dumb black basketball players are," said Bruce, seventeen years old and heading to college, "I used to join in the laughter, you know, not to make waves. Then I'd think about what they meant and I'd get mad, an hour later maybe. I'd get so annoyed that it took an hour of slamming the basketball to get rid of my frustration."

Bruce had walked away with the unsettling annoyance and anger and would carry it with him. He had to figure out a way to dump his "garbage." So he decided to take a stand, and the other kids got the message. He doesn't have to listen to prejudicial put-downs anymore.

"Now when I hear one, I say, 'I don't like that joke. It's not true for most of us, so don't tell it.' That's usually enough to cut it out."

Another way to fight prejudice is to expose others to the uniqueness of your heritage. Some groups and organizations have cultural exhibits, like the Italian-Americans or the

Native Americans. Letting others see your specialness is a move in a positive direction rather than constantly reacting to a negative mode.

"Our high school tries hard to keep the different cultures blended rather than separate," said Beverly, a Puerto Rican and a sophomore in an inner-city school. "But we also have ethnic months when one group displays its artwork, language posters, and whatever else makes it different. The cafeteria serves that group's food specialties for a week. The kids in that ethnic group sponsor a dance with their music. It's a lot of work, but we find out the good stuff to help keep out the prejudice. I like it."

Hard work is the key ingredient. Exposing others to your culture, customs, and the uniqueness of your heritage takes courage, effort, and patience. By sharing your background and showing that you have pride in your culture, you can educate others and win some of the battles in the war on prejudice.

You'll also have to accept the fact that there will always be diehards who don't want to change their minds or their prejudices. Those people are not worth your time. If they insist on making racial slurs, you have choices in how to deal with them. Like Bruce, you can say, "I don't like that. It's not true, and I want you to stop."

That will work in dealing individually or with a small not-so-threatening group. However, if you are surrounded by a pack of bullies who want to use you to bolster their own insecurities, you may want to leave the situation quickly and not waste your efforts on people who have a different agenda from yours.

Besides racial verbal abuse and prejudice, there are also social class rifts: rich and poor, the money side of town and the plain people, the snobs and the down-to-earths.

"My girlfriend's family has a lot of money. She broke

up with this rich kid and started dating me, whose family income probably couldn't buy her car," said Ronnie, a junior in high school. "Her old boyfriend always had something to say when I walked by his friends in school, really derogatory stuff."

Ronnie had choices. He could have gotten drawn into the ex-boyfriend's verbal abuse. At first he tried to ignore it, but as the romance blossomed, the abuse got worse.

"Finally, one day in the cafeteria in front of about fifty kids, the guy yells out, 'How do you like your rich girlfriend driving you around in her Ferrari, you poor slob?' At first I wanted to smash his face in, but that was probably what he wanted. It would give him an excuse to beat me to a pulp. I counted to five, then I gave him a big smile and said, 'I like it!' All the other kids laughed, and the joke was on him. Maybe I created a worse enemy, but it felt good and I didn't have to take his crap that day."

What about the subtle abuse? Smart versus dumb, pretty vs. ugly, popular vs. nerd? How do you handle that?

Many schools, in efforts to serve the needs of all the students, provide classes that range from Talented and Gifted to special education. That does help place students in their ability level, but it also creates a class system. And as much as educators call these classes by many names, they still are classes for "the brains" and "the retards."

"I have a reading problem," said Keith, a hulking football player and a member of special ed classes. "In elementary school the other kids teased us and said things. It's tough in high school being in what everyone calls the 'retard' classes. I'm pretty good in football, so they like me for that and it stops some of the teasing."

Being in the "retard" or "dummy" classes brings on some verbal abuse. People who are insecure need to bolster their self-esteem and unfortunately choose to do so by picking on other kids. You can overcome that by acting on your positive attributes. You can join sports, clubs, become part of a rock band, or do whatever you can to give yourself another identity. Capitalizing on your strong points and being recognized for them will make you feel better about yourself, increasing your self-esteem.

Then there's the other end of the spectrum. "I get so sick of the comments about the geek, the brain, the nerd. Everyone sees me only by my IQ and not the real me," lamented Jeff, a member of his school's Gifted class. "I'm not a freak, but some kids want to put me in that category and keep me there for their fun."

Jeff wins every award for academics, and his classmates are a bit jealous and probably intimidated. He needs to communicate to them that he is not so different and would like to be a friend instead of the scapegoat they set him up to be.

Jeff might do team or group things with some of the kids from his school. He could also put his feelings into words with, "I don't like it when you make fun of my grades. Cut it out."

The reality of life, however, is that there are always kids who abuse others and kids who end up being abused. You can put your energies into gaining success in other ways outside of school, to bolster your self-esteem. Working your way up to the coveted Eagle Scout honor is hard work and satisfying. Run for president of your church or synagogue youth group, or organize a blood donor drive or meals for shut-ins. Volunteer at your local hospital or nursing home, spreading cheer and companionship to needy people.

Reaching out in other ways to tap your potential and help others at the same time can help you to laugh off verbal taunts. You know that you are accomplishing good things and helping people. The slurs of immature kids lessen in importance as your own self-esteem grows.

Jody, fifteen, lost the use of his legs after a car hit him while he was riding a bike. He's had to confront and overcome those who treated him as an oddity, someone who doesn't fit in.

"I got into wheelchair racing because I needed a goal," he said. After extremely hard work, Jody became a national medal-winning racer and appeared in a commercial for Apple Computers. But he still doesn't want others to see him as abnormal. "I just say that I'm the same as they are, only a little shorter."

Handicapped people often receive ridicule and joking comments from unfeeling people. These "jokers," for some reason, need to point out the unfortunate results of the handicap. Hurtful words sear upon impact, but many handicapped people have worked on mastering these putdown people. Ignoring the ignorant verbal abusers who poke fun at their limitations is usually best. In fact, feeling sorry for the abuser, who is really humiliating himself, is common. It does no one any good to take the comments to heart and dwell on the anger.

Do you think that you are the only "uncool" kid in the world? You like old-fashioned music instead of heavy metal, and you dress for comfort rather than in black leather? Guess what? You are not alone. One girl started her own Uncool Club and organized bowling parties, hayrides, and museum trips. After posting announcements on the school's bulletin board, she found ten other "uncool" kids who enjoyed the same things she did. They had their own brand of fun while creating friendships to boot.

So you can believe the racial, social, or other prejudiced abuse flung at you. You can take it to heart, hang onto it, and live it, smoldering with resentment and hurt. Or you can turn it around to work for you. What do you say?

CHAPTER ◇ 12

Bully Abuse

Y ou see it in the newspapers: "GANG WAR RAGES OUT OF CONTROL" or "LONE TEENAGER ATTACKED BY GROUP OF SCHOOLMATES." Many against one. Bullies. Meeting a bully, in a group or alone, can be a frightening, devastating experience.

Bullies don't always use brute force. Mainly they stick to taunts, horrendous comments, and threats.

"For some reason this kid in my class needed someone to pick on, and I guess I was elected," said Josh, an eighth grader. "He'd say things real loud so everyone else could hear. Things like what a wimp I was, how stupid I was, and then he'd trip me or knock my books off my desk, and everyone would laugh."

Josh was the victim of a bully who made sure that other people saw and heard what he did. That's the modus operandi—loud verbal abuse, followed frequently by minor physical abuse such as pushing and shoving. The bully needs to feel big, and he or she achieves that by putting others down or making the victim fearful. It's a power trip for many of them, triggered by feelings of insecurity, unlovability, or other factors in their own lives that are out of their control.

You can be bullied by kids you know or by strangers on the street. Have you ever walked down a city street and come upon a group of older teenagers? Was your heart gripped with fear as you crossed the street to avoid being a victim for their verbal abuse?

Sometimes the bully uses a flimsy excuse to verbally or physically abuse others. In junior high or high school the following situation is common.

"This girl I liked last year started calling me last week," fifteen-year-old Luke said. "Out of the blue I get these phone calls. I don't even like her anymore. Then she stopped calling me, so I forgot about it. Then it all happened."

The "it" that happened was that the girl had used Luke to make her boyfriend jealous. In calling Luke and pretending to begin a relationship, she triggered a jealous anger in the boyfriend, who decided that Luke needed to be beaten up. (Someone had to be blamed for the problem.)

Luke started receiving threatening phone calls from friends of the other boy. In the halls at school he'd hear, "Billy's gonna get you and beat you to a pulp," and "If you show your face in the cafeteria tomorrow, Billy's gonna mash it in."

"I didn't know what to do," Luke admitted. "I was mostly afraid of being suspended from school. The crazy thing was that I never did anything! *She* called *me* up and then told Billy some stupid story about us, and now I was the one with the problem. What do I do if and when Billy jumps me in the hall or on my way home from school?"

Luke does have a dilemma. Bully abuse is scary and often out of our control. Sometimes you never speak directly to the bully. His or her friends are only too willing to pass along the threatening messages.

But then you see the bully walking menacingly toward you. Your friends say they'll stick by you and help you fight if you want. You want to save your pride and not be called chicken for running away. How do you handle it?

First of all, bullies usually use words rather than fists. They'll push or shove once in a while, but it's up to you to try to defuse the situation. You can try to reason things out in a nonthreatening talk with the bully (and not in front of his friends or yours).

Talking to the principal or guidance counselor can alert them to the situation. If they know that a fight may break out, they can make plans to calm things down. Perhaps having someone talk to the bully will convince him or her that a brawl won't do and that cooling off would be better for everyone.

In a head-to-head meeting with the bully, a loud "I have no reason to fight you!" might save you some grief. Keeping a low profile, walking with friends, and avoiding the bully's hangout can hold off trouble until things blow over. And usually they do. Attention shifts to other kids and events, and you lose the status of being the center of the bully's attention.

What about those of you who always seem to be the victim, the one picked on constantly by the pushy kids at school or in the neighborhood? Are you a frequent target or scapegoat of someone's frustration or vindictiveness? How do you get yourself in those situations, and how do you get yourself out?

Nydia Preto, M.S.W., is director of an adolescent care center and also works with teenagers in private practice. She says that some kids are always victims and easy marks for verbal abusers. These kids give off signals that somehow say, "Pick on me."

"In my practice, kids who are constant victims work well

in group therapy. They need a safe place to confront the position that they take as victim. These teens need to talk about what kind of situations make them feel like victims or scapegoats and what they get out of it. Because they do get something out of it. There is a function that it plays."

Kids who are easy targets need to examine what is important to them in this role as a victim. What is it that you get out of being in that position? Attention? Friendship based on negativity? Confirmation that you are an unworthy individual? What really makes sense about putting yourself in that kind of position time after time?

"I wanted friends so badly when I moved here," said thirteen-year-old Sam, "that I joined the first group that noticed me. They were kind of reject kids, but I was feeling a little rejected too after my parents' divorce and selling our house. I guess since I was small and puny, I was an easy target."

Sam took the verbal abuse of his new "friends" as a sign that they wanted him to be part of their crowd. When they pushed him around and made scathing remarks about how little and weak he was or that he was ugly or smelled bad, he figured that even though they made fun of him they accepted him. They kept him in their group as their scapegoat, and Sam felt that at least he belonged some-where. He wasn't alone, no matter how badly they treated him.

"The guys let me do a lot of things for them. I did their homework sometimes, even when they'd yell at me if it didn't get a good grade. I'd buy them stuff at lunchtime, and they let me hang out with them at the mall," said Sam.

Because Sam wanted friends, he accepted abuse as a return for the friendship that he was giving to the group. But what was Sam actually giving to the group?

Sam had put himself in the position of doormat and

scapegoat. He allowed himself no definition of "self," but gave up that function to this group of verbal abusers. He never took the position, "I don't like this" or "I want to do that."

Sam finally realized that he needed help when his "friends" set him up to buy drugs for them. He was caught at school and suspended, the police got involved, and he was recommended to therapy and counseling.

Sam learned that he came to the group full of negative feelings about himself. He felt abandoned by his mother, who didn't want him after the divorce, and by his father, whom he lived with but rarely saw. Sam lost what few friends he had by moving to another town and another school, and his self-esteem dipped below zero.

Through counseling, Sam found ways to cope with the changes in his life. He went on an inward search of how he really felt about himself. As he worked to feel better about himself, what the verbal abusers said wouldn't matter so much and he wouldn't need them to define who he was.

Sam had to learn to break away from these "friends" because he still attended the same school. By realizing that he had ingratiated himself with them in order to be accepted, he was better able to see when he was putting himself in that position and to avoid those situations. He also had to learn to be more assertive and protect himself verbally when someone sent him some real zingers.

Sam learned to like himself more and to look to the future. He started growing taller and began to work out with weights so that his mental image of himself as a "squirt" changed. All of these things helped Sam to be more in control of his life. Counseling helped, but only because he was ready and willing to self-search and improve his life.

*   *   *

What about the verbal abuse of bullies who enjoy mud-dying your sexual identity? Some such comments are made as jokes ("Hey, no harm done, right? I was just kidding.") or made in anger or ignorance. This form of bully abuse treads on the tender sexual identity that you are still working on. To have it dragged out into the open in the cafeteria or on the street—that makes you you want to crawl into a hole and never come out.

"Hey, guys, check out this fag!"

"You look like such a slut in those clothes."

"What's the matter, sweetie? You don't like boys? You only like girls?"

"Come on, honey. If you liked me, you'd go all the way. Be a real woman."

"Look at that body. Wouldn't mind taking that for my own."

Sex talk is everywhere. Television, song lyrics, and magazine ads all want to make us see the "real world" as one big sex show. The suggestive techniques of Hollywood and the music video scene are reaching down to the seven- and eight-year-olds, who think nothing of singing along with the latest Billy Idol and the Sex Pistols songs and suggestively gyrating their pelvises to the music.

Teenagers have to sort through a maze of images, seeking what is real and what is fiction. Discovering one's own sexuality and being comfortable with it takes understanding and maturity.

In this world where sex is openly discussed and flaunted by the media and, yes, in real life too, how can teenagers cope with the sexual innuendos and taunts that are directed to them each day in the halls at school and on the street?

Girls especially are the victims of sexual verbal abuse. Young girls who are still unsure of their bodies and their sexuality suffer from these attacks.

"I started in a new school my freshman year. I resolved to be friendly and say hello to people so I could make a lot of new friends," Cassie said. "My plan backfired. It turned out that most of the boys were more interested in my bra size, and my hellos were a come-on to them. They called me 'party girl,' and on my first date with a popular boy his hands tried to get some action right away. It took me a long time to get rid of that image, and it ruined my first year in that school."

Sexual taunts and nicknames can be humiliating for an adolescent who has not worked out all the answers to his or her sexual identity questions. Having to defend yourself against sexual innuendos is very difficult.

"I'm an artist, and I have five sisters, so it's easier to talk to girls than to the macho athletic guys in my school," soft-spoken Jon revealed. "So the he-man squad decided that I was gay. When I walked into to the lunchroom, this one group would lisp and flip their wrists, pointing to me. I stopped eating in the lunchroom, but they wouldn't leave me alone."

Being the butt of sexual jokes or being labeled something you're not is frightening and demoralizing. How do you live with it? What can you do about it?

First and foremost, take a look at the person flinging the sexual verbal abuse. Is it a stranger? A friend? Your sister? Your boyfriend or girlfriend? Then you need to decide whether or not to take action.

Probably the hardest thing is to take no action. "I can't let them get away with that! Everyone will think I'm gay!" (or a whore, or frigid, etc.). Entering into a heated defense of your sexuality during Spanish class may only call more attention to the nuances. "The lady doth protest too much, methinks," is an often-quoted line from Shakespeare. The more you deny the bully's allegations, the more you call attention to the labels being put on you.

Within a few days the heat will die down, because a bully or a verbal abuser likes to see the victim squirm and fight back. The bait is dangled, and if you swallow it you are hooked into exactly what the bully wants, open warfare.

If you are seriously concerned, you can speak to some of the "right" people—your close friends, or some trustworthy aquaintances whose opinion you value. You can make a comment such as, "I can't believe the trash Jerome is spreading about me. I wasn't even at that party. I guess he needs some excitement in his life and gets it by making up disgusting stories. It must be my turn this week." Those who know you will take your cue and pass your message on.

Sometimes you'll have to take stronger action. You might ask a classmate to a party where you know the bully will put in an appearance. Explain the situation to your friend. "Listen, Marsha is spreading gossip about me to some people I care about. Would you help me out? I need to show up with a date, and a popular one at that, to help fend off more of her garbage. I could use your support."

Give others a chance to know the real you, and they will soon see that the windbag is dumping on you only because he or she feels insecure about something—possibly his or her own sexuality—and needs an immediate victim.

What if the sexual taunts come from strangers? Did you ever sit in the movies and have some strange kids park themselves behind you and start making comments? Change seats, and if the harassment gets worse complain to the management. They like to keep the peace in their theaters, so they'll help.

Walking in the mall seems to put you in a vulnerable position for sexual slurs, especially girls. Go with an older brother or sister, or ask your parents to stay close as you make the rounds of the stores. Never strike up a conversation with an abuser. Walk away from that kind of situation as fast as you can.

Bearing up under a bully's pressuring taunts is no easy thing. You need to keep your cool and remind yourself that these strangers, acquaintances, or "friends" have no control over you unless you let them. They are of little importance in your life. If they have problems, you can even feel sorry for them.

If the harassment gets so bad that you fear being hurt or beaten up, get help from someone who has more resources to handle an out-of-control situation. It is not a sign of cowardice to protect yourself. It is the smart thing to do.

CHAPTER 13

Verbal Abuse

on the Job

"**I** remember my first job. I was a maid at a beach motel. I was excited to finally be making a little money. Well, I was paired up with this older woman who really took advantage of me. Now that I look back, I didn't know how to handle her comments and her abuse," said Jenny, who is sixteen and a hard-working student.

"We were supposed to take turns vacuuming the rooms, but she would look at the dirtiest rooms full of beach sand and say, 'It's your turn to vacuum.' And even though it wasn't, I just kept my mouth shut and vacuumed. She always told me I wasn't working hard enough and to quit loafing—stuff like that. She even accused me of stealing her tips when I picked up a penny from the floor after someone checked out."

Jenny stuck with the job, hating it more every day, but following the theory that adults are to be respected and she should be glad to have the job. But the situation took its toll. Doing the bulk of the heavy work for the pair, Jenny lost weight and a lot of respect for her elders. She was taken advantage of and verbally abused by this woman for the entire summer.

Kids wait years to get their first real-paycheck job. It means money, independence, and accomplishment. The rude awakening comes when you discover that you are the victim of verbal abuse from:

- your employer,
- your manager or supervisor,
- your coworkers,
- the customers.

HANDLING YOUR ABUSIVE EMPLOYER

In most jobs that teenagers fill, the owner or employer is not always present. Usually you are directly responsible to a manager or supervisor while the employer puts in occasional appearances. If this is your situation, what do you do when on his or her infrequent visits to the premises the owner indulges in demeaning tirades at you?

This is the person who signs the paycheck and who has the power to fire you. How do you react? How do you keep your job in spite of an overbearing and abusive employer?

Mark kept out of his way. "I worked one summer with a construction company building houses. The main man was the contractor, but I worked under the site supervisor. A couple of times each day the contractor came by to see how far we had gotten and if things were going according to plan. He'd drive up in his Cadillac, smoking this fat cigar, and start yelling before he even got both feet out of the car."

Fortunately for Mark, the site supervisor took most of

the verbal abuse, but the contractor made it a point to harass each of the workers at least once a day.

"I guess he thought we'd speed up if he called us lazy slobs and told us that we were stealing his money by working so slowly. I was shook up the first time he did it to me, but I learned by watching the other guys. They ignored him, never talked back, and kept on working. If a guy talked back to him or argued, he'd be fired. Maybe it was an example for the rest of us, I don't know. At least the supervisor was okay. If he had been like the the contractor, I'd have quit."

By following the lead of others, Mark learned to handle the abuse his employer doled out. He recognized that it was an attempt to unnerve the workers under the false idea that it would make them work harder and faster.

FENDING OFF A NOT-SO-SUBTLE SUPERVISOR

How about when the supervisor or manager to whom you are directly responsible is an abuser? Do you tell her where to get off, or do you bite your tongue?

If you've made a mistake on the job, you can own up to your error, putting on your ADULT perspective, and work things out with your manager. If you are being unfairly blamed for something, wait until everyone simmers down before confronting your manager. Protesting loudly during an argument, no matter how innocent you are, never gets you anywhere. Bring in your corroborating evidence to clear your record after the steam dissipates.

"My boss went on a rampage one night. Three of us share a register, and it came out thirty dollars under," said seventeen-year-old Josh. "It didn't seem fair that she screamed at all three of us when it probably was only one who made the mistake. Her behavior was terrible, and I wanted to tell her off right then and there."

Instead, Josh and the two other cashiers double-checked the receipts and over-ring slips and found the mistake. They all returned to their manager, proved the error, and the one responsible owned up.

"I think we handled it in a mature way, but we told her we didn't like her yelling at us in front of the customers. We reminded her that this was the first time we had had a problem. We apologized for the mistake and then asked her to apologize for the way she treated us."

Did the manager apologize?

"Well," Josh grinned, "she stuttered a bit and tried to get out of it, but finally she said she wouldn't get so upset next time. We told her there wouldn't be a next time."

Handling people who have authority over you takes a calm manner and an ADULT response to their verbal abuse. Getting into a shouting match and quitting is only cutting off your nose to spite your face.

If you feel strongly about quitting, quietly look for another job before thumbing your nose at your boss. A new employer may ask why you left your old job or whether you were fired; they may even call your last place of employment for references. So leave on a smooth note so the recommendations are favorable.

COPING WITH COWORKERS

Dealing with coworkers is a little tricky. One of the people who works with you is driving you crazy but you don't know what to do about it. How do you keep a job that you really like and still keep your sanity?

First assess the problem. Is he doing something illegal, or is he just bugging you with personality quirks?

Nate worked at a gas station after school. He noticed when he worked the weekend evening shift that two of the attendants made him change his pump assignment every half hour. The other days he worked he stayed at the same pump for his whole shift.

"I finally figured out that they were charging customers a dollar or two more than they had pumped. Most people don't watch the pumps or the total amount. So they'd pocket a few dollars here and a few there. It probably added up to $30 or $40 more a night," Nate said.

They moved him to other pumps so that if the customers caught on, no one could prove that they had done it. They bullied and abused Nate, who was interested in keeping the job. But as his suspicions grew, the abuse became threats.

"These guys were seventeen," said Nate, who is fifteen. "They said they'd beat me up if I didn't keep my mouth shut or they'd blame me for the stealing if we were caught. I didn't know what to do."

Threatening bullies who are quite capable of carrying out the nasty things they say can immobilize you. Do you do the "right" thing and tell the boss, risking injury or other retaliation?

Nate talked it over with a friend who worked the week-end day shift at the same station. He requested a change on the grounds that he could ride to work with the friend. His boss asked him if there were any problems on the night shift, and surmised for himself that there were. Nate was moved to a different shift and no longer had to deal with the abusive pair. They were caught eventually and did not carry out their threats against Nate.

Some decisions are difficult to make. Nate could have gone directly to his boss and told him what was happening. That seemed too much of a risk, so he decided to leave the situation by changing shifts. There's not always only one "right" way to do things.

Sometimes coworkers are just pains in the neck. They talk too much or distract you from your job. Maybe you have to cover for their mistakes, or even wind up being blamed for a problem they caused. They may use insults or verbal abuse to camouflage their own ineptness, and you'll have to take a stand at some point.

Find a time to speak to them privately. If you confront them in the presence of others, they'll be forced to save face by running you down some more. Take them aside and tell them that you don't like what they are doing or saying and to cut it out. Avoid giving them an ultimatum or you'll be drawn down to their level of abusive behavior.

If they continue the abuse you can change shifts, change departments, or even change your place of employment. Strangers who become your coworkers do not always respond to your messages because they have little invested in your mutual relationship, so you'll have to decide what steps to take. Remember that they are not important to you in the long run.

You can also enlist the aid of a sympathetic supervisor. Explain in a calm, rational way that you and your coworker do not get along and that teaming you up with someone else would be more productive for the business. Supervisors are usually aware of friction and of workers who are not well liked or effective in their performance.

CUSTOMER ABUSE

"Ugh! I worked one week in the returns department of a store at the mall right after Christmas. I never want to do that again!" wailed Julie, a senior in high school. "I never met such rude adults in my whole life! The policy of the store was to accept most returns, but the line was drawn in extreme cases. For instance, one woman brought back a dress she said she got as a Christmas present. It had been worn several times and had stains on it. She said it was too small and she had never worn it. Boy, did she say nasty things to me!"

Being on the front line where "the customer is always right" can really try your patience. Many of the jobs that teenagers have these days are in service businesses where customer satisfaction is the ultimate goal. How do you handle ugly comments or irrationally abusive customers?

"I smile a lot," revealed Maryanne, who is a waitress at a busy truckstop. "The people want their food fast with no mistakes, and when I smile and act friendly they don't snap at me as much."

"Speak quietly and clearly on an adult level with your customers," advised Billy, a summer employee at a retail chain store. "The grown-ups want to treat you like a dumb kid, so I zap them with my sophisticated routine."

"Most people who come in here are on the defensive, especially the senior citizens," said Angela, a part-time worker in a social security office. "They don't like the kids telling them what to do. Actually all you need to do is listen and act as if you *want* to help them. Then they don't have to be suspicious of you."

When you have a job, you are the link between your employer and the public. You won't last long if you drive away customers or bad-mouth them, even if they are acting worse than the school bully. Sometimes adults treat teenagers like children who aren't capable of much, and that carries over to the world of work.

"Delivering auto parts to repair shops sounded like an easy job for me," Don said. "I drove around supplying all these places with parts they had ordered."

Don found out there was pressure involved in the job. The store owners needed the parts fast, since repairs had to wait until the right piece was delivered.

"I made a few mistakes and had to go back on my own time. I did that to one owner two days in a row, and boy, did he let me have it! I had screwed up, but the language he used to tell me what an inept kid I was turned the air blue. I told my boss I wasn't going back there. He said fine, pick up your check and leave the keys—that he was sorry I didn't work out. I said whoa, I wasn't quitting, but he said if I didn't go back, I was gone."

Don had to find a way to smooth over the problem he had created. He asked his boss if he could deliver to the abusive shop owner first thing every morning. He called the owner every day to double-check the parts ordered so no more mistakes were made. A little extra effort finally changed the owner's mind about Don.

"That was the hard thing. He thought I was a jerk, a stupid kid who couldn't get anything right. I know I'm not like that, but I felt, who was this guy? He didn't count. But he counted to my boss, so I had to show him I could handle the job. There was some pride tied up in it too."

Pride. Of course. We all want to be respected and liked. That's human nature. When customers insult you and send you messages about their opinion of you, you have a choice. You can stick with the knowledge that you are a capable person or you can listen to their criticism and nasty comments and make yourself miserable.

You don't have to listen to it. Remember the rolling trashcan from Chapter 1? Dump the garbage in there and throw it out later. Look for the good in people. You are not responsible for their outlook on life. With customers, you have little time to change their view of the world, so send them positive, ADULT messages in spite of the trash they may send you. Then let go of it. You don't need to take on their disillusionment and anger. That's their problem, not yours.

CHAPTER 14

Self-inflicted

Verbal Abuse

In addition to the thousands of verbal assaults we encounter from others, self-inflicted verbal abuse happens often. We begin to believe what others say, especially those with authority over us such as parents and teachers, and those beliefs become our accepted truths.

"I am such a klutz!"

"That dress won't look well on me. I'm too fat. I can't wear nice clothes."

"Don't give me the money. I always lose it."

"You'd better find someone else to do that. I'm not very good at getting things done on time."

"God, I hate myself. I'm so ugly!"

"Nothing ever works out for me."

"I'm not like the kids around here. I have no friends."

"I can't talk to strangers. I'll just put my foot in my mouth as I always do."

"Bad luck is the only luck I have."

"Every time I lose a few pounds, I gain them right back."

"Nobody loves me!"

"I'm never on time."

"I will never be a success, no matter what happens."

"This will never work, so why bother trying?"

"My hair never goes the way I want it to."

"I'm never going to make the team, so why bother trying out?"

"All my teachers pick on me. It's not my fault."

"Me run for Student Council? Are you kidding? I'd never win!"

Where do all these personal put-downs come from?

An infant growing up through toddlerhood and into childhood does not form many opinions about himself without the help of others. Perhaps you heard a parent compare you with other children, saying that you didn't read as early as another. ("I'm stupid. I can't read.")

Or your older brother or sister made fun of your attempts to play soccer. ("If John thinks I'm a klutz, I guess I am.")

Schools, teachers, and classmates contribute much to your faltering opinion of yourself with unspoken signs that you are not capable and taunts about being a dummy.

"I was always a big kid," said Jim, six feet three and still growing in the tenth grade. "Even back in second and third grade people expected more of me than of the smaller kids. I couldn't cry if I got hurt, or I was supposed to behave better, more grown-up, just because I was bigger. So I started telling myself the same things—you're too big for this or too big for that. Now I can't stop telling myself. I'd like to act my age, not my height."

Mary Ellen had a similar problem. "I learned to play the

piano when I was four. Right away I was into piano lessons and recitals to adults. I didn't get to be a kid very much. It's like I skipped over childhood. I had to keep telling myself that I was older, that I couldn't play because I had to practice all the time. I had to keep telling myself that play was baby stuff and I wasn't a baby—I was too good for that. I told myself a lot of lies."

Jason's older brother was a high school dropout. Jason himself had been held back in third grade and heard from his brother that he was even stupider than his brother was. Jason started expecting less and less of himself, letting himself off the hook by saying, "I'm not smart at all. I can't learn much. Probably I won't finish high school." Jason had convinced himself so completely that on his sixteenth birthday he left school.

Whether you perpetuate the habit of putting yourself down is up to you. Everyone is entitled to his own opinion, but you don't have to believe every comment people send your way.

It's very difficult to live your life under a barrage of insults or even subtle remarks about your limitations by your parents and family. The psychology books say that parents should encourage and praise their kids, but in reality that doesn't always happen. Lots of kids grow up forming their self-opinion based on erroneous information.

"I always thought I was too fat," said eighteen-year-old Laura. "My mother is very petite and always dieting. When I was little she'd moan when we'd shop for school clothes about the big sizes I had to take."

Laura became so obsessed with her weight that it became an emotional problem culminating in anorexia. She dieted and exercised so much that she became skin and bones. It took a long time and much counseling for her to realize that it was okay to be big-boned like her father and to love herself for herself, rather than her distorted image of what she should be.

"My mother tells me I'm so fat," said Pauline, a seventeen-year-old. "I know it's because she's fat too and she wants me to hurt the way she's hurting. It's making me crazy! I go on all kinds of diets and then pig out again. I guess she's right. I'll never be skinny like girls in the magazines."

Pauline echoes many teenagers' concern with weight. Kids can be cruel. Parents can be cruel when they constantly point out your overweight. But when you become obsessed by what others say, you begin to believe that being thin is the only way to be happy and you become preoccupied with getting "skinny."

When does dieting become an obsession, and when does this obsession become a disease? Anorexia nervosa is a disease that strikes one out of every 250 adolescent girls in the United States. These girls, and some young men too, are starving themselves so that their body will reflect their distorted image of themselves.

Where did they get this vision of how they should be? Messages have been sent to many anorexics, quite a few in the form of verbal abuse, that they are not "perfect" or lovable if they are fat. So they starve themselves striving for the thinness that will bring them perfection and love.

Sometimes your beliefs can make you seriously depressed. Hearing over and over that you are no good can chip away at your self-esteem. After a while it becomes easier to believe what you are told rather than fighting to keep your own strengths alive.

"My father, usually when he was drunk, would say to me, 'You're good for nothing. I don't want you around. Sometimes I wish you'd disappear or go kill yourself,'" said a student who asked to remain anonymous. "I thought about killing myself plenty of times because he never let up and that was pretty heavy stuff to lay on a sixteen-year-old."

Fortunately, this boy was able to talk with a counselor and to join Alateen, a group that helps teenagers deal with alcoholic parents. He was once more able to believe in himself and his own self-worth after working his way through the verbal abuse.

Don't turn the verbal abuse of others onto yourself and help them shoot holes in your self-image. Seek out places where you can get help dealing with the problem.

Some kids give in and accept the verbal abuse as truth. The put-downs become the way to be—irresponsible, untrustworthy, etc.—and they seek a way to cover up the hurt and pain that they feel. They starting drinking and experimenting with drugs that anesthetize the pain but never ever solve the problem. Falling into this trap causes more problems, and so the cycle continues and worsens. Discover yourself! Get away from so-called friends who use you as a scapegoat. Seek out friends who have sensitivity and will understand you.

If the verbal abuse comes from your siblings, negotiate through a family conference a way to change their comments into positive statements or stop the taunts.

Listen to yourself. Are you the worst one when it comes to putting yourself down? How many times a day do you criticize things you think, do, or say? What can you do to change yourself into your own personal cheerleader?

Stop.
Look.
Listen.
Reprogram.

STOP—Make a resolution to stop the put-downs you've been heaping on yourself. You don't want them or need them.

LOOK—Really look into your life at what is making you unhappy about yourself. What do you most feel that you'd like to change? What garbage do you want to throw out and never have to deal with again?

LISTEN—Tune in to your self-inflicted verbal abuse. Practice listening to your own negative messages about yourself. Wear an elastic band around your wrist for a couple of weeks, and give it a snap when you hear yourself saying negative personal "truths". SNAP! OUCH! That hurt, didn't it? That's what you do to your mind and your heart every time you self-inflict negative verbal abuse.

Steven Schure, M.S.W., works with many teenagers in his private practice. "Not all kids suffer horrendous criticisms from their parents or verbal abuse from their siblings. Some kids just don't have strong egos. They don't believe in themselves and are the worst ones at putting themselves down," says Schure.

Working with kids who self-inflict verbal abuse, Schure uses a charting system that gives practical and immediate results in a reward system. When an adolescent has little confidence and is giving up on trying to achieve, he or she needs some success in life. Schure works out a chart with the kid and the parents to begin a success pattern.

"First we set up five things that the kid needs to do to learn to work for goals. Three of the goals may be fairly easy, such as getting to school on time or doing homework," Schure explains. "The other two should be more difficult, but tailored to some problem the kid is having—such as not wetting the bed, or not staying out late, or not yelling at the parents."

For seven days you have five goals to reach. If you

achieve your goal for the day, you can check it off on your chart. It's possible to achieve thirty-five checks by the end of the week, but you don't have to reach for perfection right away. The reward system can be worked out with your parents.

For instance, when Kevin, one of Schure's teenage clients, earned between fifteen and twenty-two checks, his parent had to take him to the stock car races on Friday night. That was something Kevin loved and wanted to achieve. If he earned between twenty-two and thirty checks, he not only went to the races but received five dollars to spend there.

If Kevin really worked on achieving his goals and turning his losing attitude around by earning from thirty-one to all thirty-five checks on his chart, he got the races and the spending money and had $10 taken off a debt he owed to the school for damages he had done to a classroom.

This chart system can help you turn around your down-and-out attitude about yourself. Maybe you were acting out because you really hated yourself and couldn't stand the unhappiness anymore. Maybe you feel that you can't do anything right or that your parents wouldn't notice if you did. The chart can work for you!

In his book *What to Say When You Talk to Yourself*, Dr. Shad Helmstetter writes that each of us has a powerful personal computer in our brain. This computer is programmed with information that will work for us the way that we tell it to work. If we feed our computer negative stuff, that's how it will make us act. If we feed it positive stuff, that's how it will make us act.

Dr. Helmstetter states that even in a reasonably positive home with supportive parents, you'll still hear, remember, and program more than a hundred thousand negative messages as you grow up. Thinking back over your life so far, how may times were you told that you were *very* capable of being or accomplishing something? One thousand? One hundred? Ten? One? As was said in Chapter 1, it takes three positive messages to wipe out one put-down. As you grow up and hear negative messages, especially from people in authority like your parents and teachers, you'll program mostly negative stuff into your brain's computer. It will take an enormous of good data to counteract the junk. You can continue the dumping of negative data and perpetuate your poor self-image.

If you believe you cannot give a speech in front of the class, you won't be able to give that speech.

If you believe you're such a zero personality that you'll never have a girlfriend, you'll never have a girlfriend.

If you believe you're a loser, you'll never win.

Your programming has been going on your whole life. Repetitions of negative verbal messages have made it easy for you to continue this pattern. Whether true or not, you have believed those messages, usually without questioning them. The more you believe them, the more your brain will act on them to make them stay true.

As Dr. Helmstetter writes, our programming makes us believe ideas as truths. Those beliefs color the way we see things in life, either good or not so good. They arouse feelings in us, and we act on our feelings.

Joanie's parents were college professors. Since day one, she was told she was going to college. Along the way her parents made sure that Joanie had extra tutoring, expected her to memorize SAT vocabulary words, and sent her lots of messages that said, "We think you may not be smart enough to get into a good college on your own. You need all the help you can get."

Joanie heard those messages loud and clear. She picked

up on her parents' programming and added her own negative stuff to it. Her self-inflicted verbal abuse that she wasn't very smart and could never get into college on her own was repeatedly stored in her personal computer. She believed this "truth" totally.

She agonized over her college prep classes, she froze on the SATs that she started taking in seventh grade "for practice," and she flunked algebra in ninth grade. Joanie hated and feared all the preparation for college. Her feelings became so intense that she couldn't function in her classes anymore.

Joanie's grades and SAT scores were so poor that she wasn't able to get into a good college, just as her parents had predicted. They must have known all along, right? Their negative programming for Joanie became true.

What Joanie needed to do was to change her program. She needed to counteract all that subtle verbal abuse with positive data to her brain. Sounds easy, doesn't it? In reality, it requires forcing a belief in yourself and repeating the positive messages many, many times into your computer so that you can begin to believe them.

As you start off with a belief, your attitude will change and you'll start to feel good about yourself. Those good feelings will enable you to accomplish something that will make your initial belief even truer.

At first your personal message may be something like, "I really should get to school on time," or "I'd like to lose some weight, but I'm not sure I can."

Get past this stage quickly, because all the shoulds, coulds, and oughtas won't bring the desired results. The *beliefs* you want to program aren't very strong at this stage, so move on to stronger positive data.

Even though you may not believe your positive data as total truth, start repeating your personal message. It takes a lot of repetition to make a truth. Begin with, "I don't have a problem getting to school on time," or "I will be patient with my little sister today."

The data will sink into your subconscious and be programmed into your computer until it *does* become your truth. You are creating new images of yourself in your mind, and you will begin to act on those new images. You will get to school on time and you will lose weight if you *believe* your truth, not someone else's.

After you work through that stage, become your own personal cheerleader. You can empty out your old data bank and insert a new disc programming a new you!

"I am a capable person! I am a winner! I can be successful at this next endeavor!"

"I am a good speaker! My tongue stays loose and ready to wow my audience."

"I am graceful and a smooth dancer."

"I am a lovable and worthy person. I will make a good boyfriend for some lucky girl!"

Try it in your mirror. All right, close the door so no one hears you at first. Say it aloud to the person in the mirror. Do you feel awkward the first few times? After a hundred or two hundred or a thousand, it won't matter. You *will* feel lovable and successful and graceful.

Once you've got the hang of saying it, you can put it on file cards and hang them on your mirror or your headboard. That way you'll see them many times a day, from first thing in the morning to last thing at night. Get a small tape recorder and record your personal message. Add more specific details to it and play it over and over when you ride in the car or as you wash the dishes.

"There's no other person in the world exactly like me. I have special talents and abilities. I work hard to make me the best I can be each and every day. I like myself, and today is a day to make me proud!"

This won't happen overnight. Some of your negative data were programmed into you for years. But your subconscious mind will take the new direction in which you are sending it and act on the truths you now believe about yourself. Start with something small if you are nervous, then work up to some major "truths" you really want to change.

Press your button and bring up on your screen the vision of yourself that you want to be. That's the program you want to follow!

CHAPTER 15

Self-esteem

Self-esteem is your own image of yourself, how you feel about *you*, your attitude toward yourself. You have many thoughts about the person you are, which can be both positive and negative, good and not so good.

As you grow from infancy through your teenage years, you may allow others to help shape your self-esteem. Your parents, teachers, brothers and sisters, friends, boyfriend or girlfriend, and even strangers will contribute to your self-image. Through comments, compliments, insults, or verbal abuse, these others can influence what you think of yourself if you let them.

Your self-esteem is determined by the many experiences and personal relationships you've had in your life so far. Time helps you develop who you are, and that can be constantly changing with every experience you encounter.

If up to this point you have had to deal with negative relationships or verbal abuse from your parents or in other close relationships, realize that it is never too late to change and evolve into a person who thinks well of himself. If *you* want to work on this, that's the first big step. Wishing or waiting for something to happen to change your life and your perception of yourself won't do it.

You are in charge of what you think of yourself. No one else is. Don't give up your power over your own thoughts to anyone!

Yes, you say, but if everyone thinks that I'll never graduate from high school, how can I believe that I can? Remember, the first step is to want to change. Then get some help for that change. If graduating from high school is your goal in spite of what everyone says, there are different ways to accomplish it.

Perhaps you won't make it by June of your senior year. Some kids finish up in summer school or even return for a fifth year to take the classes needed for graduation. Many high schools have an adult program for those over eighteen years of age who want to get the diploma. These programs are usually more relaxed, since the classes are worked around your job schedule, and much work is done at home.

You could obtain a Graduate Equivalency Diploma (GED) and go right on to college courses. Some adult high schools give credits toward graduation for passing the GED. So there are other ways to graduate. Perhaps they don't match the vision of cap and gown in June after your senior year, but it's okay to change the vision. When you do finish, you will have a feeling of great accomplishment and you will have shown those who said you'd never make it. Your self-esteem will rise a notch or two because you have worked hard toward a goal and met it.

Self-esteem may feel like a roller coaster ride through your teenage years. Some days you look in the mirror and like what you see. Other days. . .

"I don't think I have very high self-esteem," said Susan,

a junior in high school. "Once in a while I like myself, but then someone will say something, like my sister or my boyfriend, and I'll feel ugly, stupid, unpopular."

Try to see the positive points that you possess (and you won't have to search far). You may think that you have a nice smile, that you are loyal to friends, or do well in sports. The more positive thoughts you have about yourself, the higher your self-esteem will be.

On the down side, you may think that you are clumsy, shy, boring, afraid of taking risks, or ugly. If you have mostly negative thoughts about yourself, the lower your self-esteem will be.

Vickie Wilson, who is a specially trained substance abuse counselor in New Jersey, says, "Many of the kids I see in crisis situations have very low self-esteem. It's been a downhill struggle for them for a long time, and they can't find too many things that they like about themselves."

If you've been battered emotionally or constantly put down and criticized, your self-image may be somewhat tarnished.

"I live with my grandparents," said Darcy, "and having to put up with Grandma's idea of how girls should act is driving me crazy! She's constantly harping on what I wear, how I talk, what boys I go out with. Sometimes I do outrageous things to freak her out!"

Struggling to see through to your emerging adult personality can sometimes tempt you to do "outrageous things" so your family and friends will not miss the real you. But that can backfire too. The outrageous things that some kids use to shock others into seeing them differently—such as alcohol or drug abuse, fast driving, running away, and dropping out of school—can only hurt in the long run. There are other, less self-destructive ways to make your statement.

As you try to figure out who you are becoming, pay attention to how you think about yourself. Seriously. Self-esteem affects how you think, act, and feel about yourself and others. It also affects how successful you are in achieving your goals and dreams in life.

"Many kids get feedback for their self-image from school or from their friends," says Esther Ganz, a counselor in private practice. "The importance of their peer group or boyfriend or girlfriend is great. When they lose that group or close friend, they often feel they lose everything. Their self-esteem bottoms out at zero, and some kids can't come back from that easily."

Don't hang your picture of yourself on one nail. If you tie up your identity to one person, when that one person verbally abuses you you'll believe it and lose your image of yourself. Believe in yourself. That's the key.

But how? It's easy to say but hard to do. If your mother thinks you're a terrible kid, then aren't you? Not necessarily. You can change your own thoughts about yourself. No one else defines your personality. Others can influence it *if* you let them. They can dictate who you are *if you give them that power*. But it is *your* power. You don't have to give it away.

There are things you can do for yourself to boost your self-esteem and keep you believing in yourself no matter what anyone else says.

PRAISE

Enjoy compliments, and give yourself a pat on the back for accomplishments big and small. Be proud of yourself. It's okay to tell your heart, "Wow, I really feel good about stopping and changing that old lady's tire today. I'm a nice guy!" Say that into your mirror. It's sure to bring a smile!

If someone compliments you, accept it with a "Thanks" rather than pointing out a negative thing or putting yourself down.

"I like the way you did your hair. It looks nice."

"Yeah, well, my hair is so limp and thin it won't last long like this. In an hour it'll look gross again."

That kind of thinking is like sticking a pin in your ego. You can change it. Consciously say to yourself in the mirror, "You look nice (or cute or funky or something positive)," and answer that person in the mirror giving you that compliment with a simple "Thanks." Try it!

SET GOALS

Write down some goals you'd like to reach, and give yourself a reasonable timetable to reach them. Start with two or three. Don't overwhelm yourself with a list of twenty tough goals; that only sets you up for failure and pounding your already suffering self-image to the ground. Maybe you'd like to lose five pounds, make a new friend, get a job, join the guitar group at school, enter a sporting event, or earn a B in science.

Develop the abilities and skills to reach those goals. Map out a strategy. Seek out those who can help you on your way to succeeding. Encourage yourself along the way. And tell others about your goals. It will make you want to reach them even more.

BE YOURSELF

Don't try to copy someone else. Give yourself permission to accept, trust, and respect yourself. Identify and accept your weaknesses as well as your strengths. Nobody is perfect. Everyone has faults. But don't magnify and concentrate on your weaker points. So what if you aren't athletic or funny? Rely on your own feelings and thoughts. Don't accept others' opinions of you as gospel truth. Recognize your importance, and act on what you think is right.

"I used to try out for all the teams, knowing I would get cut," said fifteen-year-old Tyrone. "It was partly to satisfy my old man, who was a big basketball player in high school. When I didn't make the team I had to hear it from my father, but then he'd let up because there was nothing he could do about it."

Tyrone went in another direction to feel positive about himself. He helped organize a peer counseling team of students who helped other kids. His strengths were that he made friends easily and was a good listener, two skills that were key qualities for a peer counselor.

TAKE TIME OUT FOR YOURSELF

Spend some time with your best friend—yourself! Blow off the pressures and the things that weigh you down with some things you can do while you are alone with your thoughts and feelings.

Maybe you like to fish. Lazing about on the bank of a peaceful stream will clear out the cobwebs and give you an opportunity to see yourself more clearly.

Kids who are into jogging, running, or other exercise do their thoughtful introspection on the move, allowing their mind to flow and fill themselves up with good feelings.

Perhaps painting, reading, dancing, motorbike riding, or another activity does it for you. Whatever you choose, it should be "me time," during which you learn to enjoy your own company. It's not being selfish. It's healthy for your mind, especially when you are under stress.

It will take time and effort to change your way of thinking. If you have believed for years that you are ugly, fat, hateful, weak, or a loser because that's what you've been told, one week is not long enough to repaint your picture. The results are worth it. If you want to change your self-image but feel overwhelmed by the prospect, seek out a counselor who can direct you on your way.

Since the way you see yourself is personal, the way you receive messages, constructive or harsh, from others is your own interpretation of you. Kids have committed suicide because they couldn't live with their own image or couldn't deal with words or attitudes that made them feel unloved.

Fending off verbal abuse and not letting it dictate who you are takes effort, but you can strengthen yourself on the road to a strong, positive self-image.

High self-esteem doesn't guarantee success, a great job, or lots of money. But you will feel so good about yourself that it will spill over to others—most important, to your family and friends. Your life will move in a positive direction with you in the driver's seat. Go for it!

CHAPTER 16

Nonabusive

Final Words

F irst of all, congratulate yourself for reading this book. You have sought help in an area of your life where you have been having some difficulty. Whether you find yourself on the giving end of verbal abuse or on the receiving end, by incorporating the suggestions in this book you will have control over another important aspect of your life.

By exploring the situations in which you find yourself involved with verbal or emotional abuse, you will be better able to identify messages that you need to listen to and those that are really other people's problems.

In the case of a bully or abusive parents, you need not take on their problems as your own. Those people who need to vent their own frustrations and failures *do not* control your self-image. Work on building your own self-esteem, and strive to be honest about yourself as you work to gain control of your own behavior.

But what if you find these tasks too difficult? You may

say, "Sure, it's easy to say I'm going to do these things, but when I actually have to, I can't." Then it's time to get some extra help.

Seeking professional help still carries some myths. No, you don't have to be crazy to see a psychologist or a family counselor. In fact, for some teens it is becoming a status symbol. "Yeah, my parents are taking me for counseling. They don't know how to deal with me anymore."

Maybe you want to take an assertiveness training workshop at your community college. School districts also offer similar courses along with computer programming and sewing classes. You might find "How to deal with anger" offered in the evenings.

When you feel that you cannot handle your problems by yourself, when you face a stressful emotional upheaval that is getting out of control, such as divorce or a death in your family, you might decide to seek one-to-one counseling.

There are different types of counselors and different types of therapy. Depending on your own choice, the cooperation of your parents, and your financial situation, you can choose the counseling that fits your needs. You might see a psychologist in private practice, a psychiatrist, a family counselor either in a clinic or privately, or a youth counselor or clergyperson at your church or synagogue.

If you (or a parent who is seeking help with you) are really baffled as to where to turn first, start with your school. Almost every school in the country has guidance counselors and a Child Study Team consisting of a psychologist, a social worker, and a learning disabilities consultant.

Set up a meeting with your counselor and perhaps the school psychologist. They will be able to assess your problem, talk with your parents, and then direct you to outside agencies or therapists where you can get help on a regular basis.

You might be referred to a mental health clinic or a family counseling agency. There you will meet trained counselors who can help you deal with your overwhelming problems. These clinics and agencies have staff members with different qualifications and degrees, and you'll be able to find someone who is empathetic and skilled to help you cope with your feelings.

You may want to go to someone in private practice. A psychiatrist is a medical doctor (M.D.), a physician who has extensive training in helping people with psychological and emotional problems. The psychiatrist can also prescribe drugs, if needed to help severely depressed people.

Perhaps a psychologist is the person to whom you choose to go for help. Psychologists have college degrees in psychology, always a master's degree, and usually a doctorate, which is the highest academic degree. Their degree work centered on clinical psychology, which means that they spent a lot of time in the field, in training and working with people with emotional problems.

Therapists with an M.S.W. (Master of Social Work) degree receive training in social work combined with the emotional aspect of social problems. Many of them have training in psychiatric social work.

Another choice could be a licensed family counselor/ therapist who has a master's degree in psychology or marriage and family counseling. Not every state has licensing procedures, so beware of someone who just hangs up a sign but is not fully qualified.

Youth centers have counselors who may not have a lot of degrees but who can offer warm feelings and strong listening and counseling skills. Your priest, minister, or rabbi also has training and experience in working with families in crisis.

No matter what diplomas hang on the wall, you need to

find a therapist whom you can trust, communicate with, and depend on to work with you in a constructive way. If you find yourself with someone who really turns you off or who starts in with a lecture and hassles you, look for a different counselor.

Ideally, a good therapist is an active listener, one who really hears what you are saying and can feed it back to you in a way that helps you face your feelings. Your therapist should not tell you what to do or try to make you accept his or her beliefs. He or she should help you find ways to face your problem and begin to make changes in your life. You need to be guided to find your own solutions.

If you can get one or both your parents involved, that's great. Many times it's the parents who want and need help. If that's the case, don't resist. Learning to share feelings and ideas on how you can achieve better family interaction is important. By having a counselor who is an impartial facilitator, your family can confront deep-seated issues that have been driving all of you apart.

Improving family communications will go a long way to curtail the need to hurt each other. You can carry over the new behavior learned in the counseling sessions into your everyday lives, thereby easing the strife.

Another form of counseling is group therapy. You'll find that there are lots of other kids who have similar problems and feelings of helplessness and hopelessness. You don't have to be alone. You can trade ideas of what works and what doesn't and lean on each other as you grow stronger and more able to cope with the tough problems in your life.

Individual counseling is also an option. Some teens would rather speak privately or feel the need for immediate, intensive therapy. Then by all means, seek out a one-to-one counseling experience.

If you are uptight and afraid to go the professional route,

you can begin anonymously by calling a crisis hotline. There trained people answer the phones, ready to listen and refer you to an appropriate place to take your problem. This cannot take the place of long-term counseling, but it can be an important first step.

How much does it cost? Money is always tight, and these suggestions may sound scary to you of the empty pockets, especially if you expect no cooperation from your parents.

Counseling can cost you nothing or could run into thousands of dollars. Special centers such as youth houses and crisis centers at the YMCA or similar organizations do not charge for services. Your minister, rabbi, or priest can offer help with no fee, as can your guidance counselor at school and the school psychologist or social worker. Some mental health clinics and family service centers charge on a sliding scale based on your ability to pay, and they some-times allow extra time for payment. These services may cost you anywhere from nothing to $40 or $50 a visit.

Some places will require you to have parental permission for treatment. Others won't. Some will want to speak to your parents and encourage them to become part of the change process. Some parents will resist, feeling that accepting counseling would mean that they can't handle your problems or that they are parental failures. Other parents will welcome the opportunity to get coping insight from a professional.

The main point is change, and that the person seeking help must *want* to change. Independence and self-reliance are important to teens, so you must be willing to work on yourself to reach the desired results. You need to make a commitment to work hard to develop the skills and the courage to change your life.

Be realistic. Seeing a therapist does not magically take away all your pain and suffering. In fact, sometimes you'll need to explore the pain and its causes in order to learn to cope with it. You don't want a counselor who will tell you what to do. You want help for *you* to work through your emotional problems, where *you* are the one who makes the decisions and finds the solutions.

Now, go to a mirror and look at yourself. Say to that reflection, "Okay, Self. I'm a worthwhile, capable, and lovable person. I can find ways to cope with my emotional problems. I am strong and willing to work. I will seek help to get me through the toughest spots. I'm all right. I will make it."

Bibliography

Bolton, Robert, Ph.D. *People Skills—How to Assert Yourself, Listen to Others, and Resolve Conflicts.* Englewood Cliffs, N.J.: Prentice-Hall, Inc., 1979.

Elgin, Suzette. *The Last Word on the Gentle Art of Verbal Self-defense.* New York: Prentice-Hall, Inc., 1987.

Gelinas, Paul J. *Coping with Anger.* New York: Rosen Publishing Group, 1983.

Harris, Thomas, M.D. *I'm OK, You're OK—A Practical Guide to Transactional Analysis.* New York: Harper & Row, 1967.

Helmstetter, Shad, Ph.D. *What to Say When You Talk to Yourself.* Scottsdale, Ariz: Grindle Press, 1986.

Kaplan, Leslie, Ed.D. *Coping with Peer Pressure.* New York: Rosen Publishing Group, 1983.

Levenkron, Steven. *Treating and Overcoming Anorexia Nervosa.* New York: Charles Scribner's Sons, 1982.

McCoy, Kathy. *The Teenage Survival Guide.* New York: Simon & Schuster (Wallaby Books), 1981.

Norwood, Robin. *Women Who Love Too Much.* Los Angeles: Jeremy P. Tarcher, Inc., 1985.

Rinzler, Jane. *Teens Speak Out.* New York: Donald I. Fine, Inc., 1985.

Satir, Virginia. *Conjoint Family Therapy.* Palo Alto: Science and Behavior Books, 1964.

———. *Peoplemaking.* Palo Alto: Science and Behavior Books, 1972.

Smith, Manuel. *When I Say No, I Feel Guilty.* New York: Dial Press, 1975.

Index